T0195059

OLD TESTAMENT STORIES *for* NEW TESTAMENT STRENGTH

DOUG ROWLAND

WESTBOW
PRESS®
A DIVISION OF THOMAS NELSON
& ZONDERVAN

WestBow Press books may be ordered through booksellers or by contacting:

WestBow Press
A Division of Thomas Nelson & Zondervan
1663 Liberty Drive
Bloomington, IN 47403
www.westbowpress.com
844-714-3454

Scripture taken from the King James Version of the Bible.

Scripture quotations are from the ESV® Bible (The Holy Bible, English Standard Version®), copyright © 2001 by Crossway, a publishing ministry of Good News Publishers. Used by permission. All rights reserved.

ISBN: 978-1-6642-1462-0 (sc)
ISBN: 978-1-6642-1463-7 (hc)
ISBN: 978-1-6642-1461-3 (e)

Library of Congress Control Number: 2020923936

Print information available on the last page.

WestBow Press rev. date: 01/13/2021

CONTENTS

After forty- five years in the ministry, God began to lead me into putting to paper some stories and some humorous situations along with strong Bible principles that I felt would help the average Christian. Proverbs 22:17 (King James Version) (KJV) states *"A merry heart doeth good like a medicine."* Even though we are in very trying times, if the inside of a person is merry, it shows up on a person's face. And of course, the same is true of an old grouchy, stick in the mud, look on the bad side of things as doom and gloom. I don't know about you, but I would rather be around a person of joy, peace and gladness than a person filled with doom, gloom and sadness any day. I do not want this to be a Christian comic book nor do I wish for it to be a commentary of scripture for a classroom in Bible College. After pastoring four churches and then in evangelism twenty-two years, I can say there is nothing in the world of Christianity that I have not seen, heard, or heard about happening that would surprise me. Serving the Lord has been a blast. I do want you to know up front, that like you, at times I have made some very bad choices in life. I often hear it said, "If I had it to do all over again, I would not change a thing." If I had my life to live over again, knowing what I know now, there are many things I would change. I did some things that were just plain from stupid 'Ville. I also see more and more the things I should have done and did not pounce on the opportunity. At the writing of this book I am sixty-three years old going on ninety. I can still stand behind the pulpit to preach, but as for walking I am now in a wheelchair. I have some health issues that hinder me from pastoring. As time has gone by, old fashion revivals have gone down at an alarming rate. But even with all the evil, sin, immorality, pain, disease and suffering, God is still on the throne and God's people ought to be full of joy and abundance. As you read thru this book you will find my jokes are corny and old more than likely. But don't tell me how bad they are, you would hurt my feelings so much......ha, ha. Some of the stories will sound like they must be made up. The jokes may be bad, but the stories are true! My goal is to write something that you will have through the good times and the bad times. For when times or months you are skipping from mountain top to mountain top. Yes, you will also have valleys so low you might have to get a ladder to reach the top. Everything you have said, done, thought, every emotion, valley, victory, or situation are not any different than what other believers have also experienced. I have really tried to cover as much that is common to all Christians as I could. Some of these chapters are sermons I have preached either as a pastor or as an evangelist. Other chapters are things that we all have faced, but really do not like to think about. I did not write this so I could brag that I am a published author. My heart's desire was to show you that we believers share the same burdens and also are serving the one true and living God, the Lord Jesus Christ.

In the early second century, Marcion, the son of a Turkish bishop, made his way to Rome. The theologically-minded wealthy shipbuilder joined the Roman church and considered himself a strong disciple of the Apostle Paul. As he studied the Scriptures, he came to the conclusion that the New Testament teachings of Jesus of Nazareth could not be reconciled with the actions of YHWH, the divine being found on almost every page of the Old Testament. Marcion began to teach there were two different "Gods" in the Jewish and Christian writings. The Old Testament God was the Creator of this evil material world and interacted with his creation in wrath, anger, and judgment. Meanwhile, the New Testament God, the Father of Jesus Christ, is a God of love, compassion, mercy, and grace. After establishing this false dichotomy, Marcion believed he was left with no option but to reject and abandon the entire Old Testament. He also eliminated any portion of the New Testament that falsely linked these two Gods together, keeping only portions of Luke's Gospel and highly edited versions of ten of Paul's letters. Believing the church had illegitimately mingled the laws of Judaism and the grace of Christianity, he preached the two distinct religions should forever be separated from one another. Likewise, the Old and New Testaments should also be kept separate and the older covenant should never be read in new covenant churches.

Marcion and his beliefs were roundly condemned by the church and he was excommunicated from the Church in Rome in AD 144. Surprisingly, Marcion still has his followers today, though all would deny such an accusation and most could not name the man who gave birth to their beliefs. Some modern-day Marcionites are quite zealous, still thinking of an angry Old Testament God of wrath and a New Testament God of love. Others are more benign, merely having a relatively low view of the Old Testament. Both exist today because of years of neglect of the Old Testament in evangelical churches. In one study, only 20 percent of all sermons preached in evangelical church have the Old Testament as the foundational text, which is exceedingly strange when you consider the Old Testament makes up over 75 percent of the Bible Some pastors neglect the Old Testament because they do not know how to study it or preach from a narrative text (or poetry). Other pastors have the naïve understanding that they serve in a "New Testament church" and therefore should only preach from the New Testament. They sometimes feel pressure from the pews to stay away from the Old Testament, which seems so irrelevant to our modern minds.

Nothing could be further from the truth. It is for that reason I am so glad Doug Rowland has produced this book. Within its pages are a collection of sermons from his preaching ministry of over 45 years. Each sermon is taken from the Old Testament, helping us to see its eternal relevance, theological depth, and practical application. You have my gratitude for doing so.

Doug has been a faithful member of the church I pastor for over three years. He came here after pastoring many church and preaching sermons in 238 other churches. That could be intimidating to a younger pastor but Doug has been a constant source of encouragement to me and to our congregation, who affectionately refer to him as "The Amen Guy." Doug has had to get around in a wheelchair since a bad auto accident years ago (which is how I came to know Doug, visiting him in a rehabilitation hospital). However, the wheelchair has not slowed him down all that much, merely forcing him to sit more than he stands when he preaches (which is still quite often). I am glad to have Doug and his lovely wife Donna in our church family and I believe his book of Old Testament sermons will be a blessing to anyone who reads them.

FN: Hebert Mayer, "The Old Testament in the Pulpit," *Concordia Theological Monthly* 35 (1964), 603, and John Stapert, *Church Herald* [Reformed Church in America], July 13, 1979, 9, as quoted in Sidney Greidanus, *Preaching Christ from the Old Testament: A Contemporary Hermeneutical Method* (Grand Rapids: Eerdmans, 1999), 15 fn 35.

— 1 —
LAME FEET NEVER HAD IT SO SWEET

2 SAMUEL CHAPTER 9

Friendship is one of those relationships that most every person on earth yearns to have. I have heard it said that if a person could name five people that are real friends you are a very fortunate person. There are several definitions of what a true 100% real friend is. The one I like the best is very simple. Someone that knows **all** about you and still chooses to like you. Not everyone that you are on a first name basis with is your friend. A person who knows all about you is one that knows your secret life and failures and what your public persona is and still sticks by you. In show business it is said Ben Affleck and Matt Damon are pals to the end . Years ago, there was a comedy duo with Dean Martin and Jerry Lewis. As long as they were together and seeing each other as often as they were you would have been bosom comrades to the end. However, one day their act broke up and did not speak to one another for I think more than twenty-five years. This leads me to two people in the Bible that were absolutely best friends in the entire definition of the word friend. 2 Samuel 1:26 (English Standard Version) (ESV) says *" I am distressed for my brother Johnathan very pleasant hast thou*

been unto me thy love to me was wonderful passing the love of women" . No this does not mean they were homosexuals. The greatest love in the world is the love of a woman to her children. Someone may be called a daddy's girl. But a man does not have the capacity for love as does a woman for her children in the human and in the animal world.

David was saying to his friend Johnathan that he loved him more than a woman does her own flesh and blood child. We find again in 1 Samuel 18 :1-3 another scripture speaks of the love and friendship that both Johnathan and David had for each other. They made a covenant with each other to take care of each other's families upon the death of either one. If you are in the category that does not believe you have any friends at all I have great news for you. I am speaking of Jesus Christ himself when he said *"Greater love hath no man than this that a man lay down his life for his friends.* In Proverbs 17:17 (KJV) the Bible says, *"a friend loveth at all time."*

That is good news for me. Though all friends may drop me the man Jesus Christ is my best friend at all times. Now to understand the story we find here in 2 Samuel 19 we must nail down the simple fact that Johnathan and David were the closest friends found anywhere in the Bible, outside of our Savior. Johnathan has a son named

Mephibosheth that lives in the house of Machir down in the land of Lodebar. Let us examine this young man Mephibosheth and then find out through the scripture and use our own imagination as to what happened to the son of his best friend. Remember we are taking Old Testament stories and seeing how they give us New Testament strength. This gives us a perfect picture of what happened when we were born again. First, let's break down this story about this character with such a long name Mephibosheth. Now I ask you, if you are a young person, would you possibly want the name Mephibosheth? My oldest daughter in Montana named all three of their natural children biblical names: Benjamin, Levi and Hannah. Three children did not seem to keep her busy enough. So, they adopted two more children and named them Judah and Sarah. But as her father, I am not sure I would have been crazy about naming little Judah, Mephibosheth. What would kids say at school? Well nothing really, they are home schooled . But what about applying for college or filling out a job application. Then would he later on in life have a Mephibosheth II or III? O my thank God for sensible children. Notice these things about Mephibosheth and then lend me your imagination for just a thought on what could have happened.

The Fall of Mephibosheth

Just remember this lad with a rad name of Mephibosheth was Johnathan's son. And that David and Johnathan had made a covenant bound by their love for each other. Jesus told the Father God that "all that comes to me I will no wise cast out". I am so glad that when we come to the Savior whether a pauper or millionaire, sick or healthy, ditch digger or king, he will not cast us out. Romans 10:13 (KJV) tells us, *"for whosoever shall call upon the name of the Lord shall be saved."* However, let us see why it was, that this young child Mephibosheth, was lame on his feet. Back a few chapters, in 2 Samuel 4:4 we find Mephibosheth staying with a nurse, when word came that a war was coming. The nurse bundled up this young man and began to flee the city. As she was fleeing, she fell with the child and he became lame on both feet.

After thinking and studying about that fall, I was not satisfied that he merely broke his legs. In biblical times, the wars were rough, and I am sure many people broke their legs during battle. But eventually broken legs, arms, even backs would eventually heal. I am asking you to think about this; maybe when he fell, a spinal injury had occurred. My reasoning was that he was lame the day he fell, even though later at the kings table he was still lame on both feet. The significance of this is simple. When Adam and Eve fell in the garden of Eden by eating the forbidden fruit, each and every person ever born since that time, was born a sinner. We cannot bind up sins' wounds with religion, works, baptism, joining a church, or giving the most money. None of those things can help the lameness of sin that all men are born into. And mankind will never get to God until he realizes his or her sinful condition. So just as Mephibosheth was lame on his feet, man in his sinful condition, is also lame in trespasses and sins.

The Feet of Mephibosheth

Since he was lame on his feet there was nothing that could be done, to undo the fact, that he was lame. He was in a bad predicament. I am sure they took him to doctors and people who made great promises of him being healed nothing would work. When Jonathan died, he must have laid away enough money so that his small son could at least, have a nurse to take care of him. However, money was not the answer. If money had been the answer to man's problems, how much would be enough? If works could save you, what works would it be? And for how long would you have to work to satisfy the demand that Romans 6:23 (KJV) requires? This verse states *"the wages of sin is death but the gift of God is eternal life through Jesus Christ our Lord"*. What can wash away my sin (lameness) nothing but the blood of Jesus. Jesus took man's sins and lameness on the cross and paid for our sin, death, hell and the grave. Just as nothing could be done for Mephibosheth; nothing can be done for or you and I but Jesus. Only Jesus could take our place on the cross!

The Famine of Mephibosheth

The Bible says that this young man was living with old evil Machir, down in what was called *the land of no bread*, in Lodebar. Nothing to eat, bramble bushes blowing down the road of nothing; but sand, dirt and rocks strewn about here and there. Later we will see that Lodebar is a picture of the world. How sad for this lad, Johnathan's son, to be living in an old mess of a town, with possibly no food walking with chains around him so he could escape. Hebrews 2:3 (KJV) *" How shall we escape if we neglect so great salvation."* The answer is there is not an escape. Dear reader, do not allow one more second of neglecting so great a salvation. Mephibosheth's home was kept by Machir, a picture of the Devil. Lodebar was a picture of the world. And just as the King brought Mephibosheth out of all that place of misery, one day Jesus pulled me out of my place of misery. He adopted me, and if you are born again, you too have been adopted by the King of Kings and Lord of Lords. What a great thought to be one of the Kings children. But

Mephibosheth was in the midst of a great famine, in an obscure land of no bread, called Lodebar.

The Fetching of Mephibosheth

I just love the way the King James Version puts this point. The Bible says in 2 Samuel 9:5 *"then King David sent and fetched him out"*. I was preaching a revival in little place in Emmorton, Maryland years ago. I came across this scripture, and I said, "and King David fetched him out of that awful place called Lodebar." After church this lady came up to me dressed like she was going to the White House for supper, and looked at me as if she was the smartest bible scholar in the world, and sanctimoniously looking at me as if I just committed first degree murder and said "Well! I do not think you should use the word fetch." I said lady, I'd rather fetch him and get him than to send for him and not get him! She turned around and waddling like a duck she left the church. I do not care how Jesus got me out of this world, as long as he gets me. The whole story is Mephibosheth was fetched out of that awful place of Lodebar. And for all of us that are born-again, he did the same for us. One day when the rapture takes place, He will fetch us from this physical world.

The Fellowship of Mephibosheth

The king had sent his servant Ziba to Lodebar, to fetch the son of Johnathan. He had remembered the covenant he had made with the one man he loved more than any other person on earth. And this little lame boy was brought back to the castle. There the boy bowed down and asked King David, why would you want such a dead dog as I? I do not know about you, but I would imagine there was a reunion to end all reunions when David began to share the story about his friendship with the lad's father, Jonathan.

Dear reader stop reading for a moment and clear everything from your mind before you read on. O.K, now that your mind is clear, think about this for a moment. You and I have the privilege to fellowship with a King. The one who spoke this world into being and it was so. He placed the stars in their sockets, and it was so. He made every single fish, bird, dog, cat, elephant and the list goes on and on and on. The whole universe was made at the mere mention of his voice. The Milky Way and the whole solar system, He spoke, and it was so. This God, that did all of this, wants to have fellowship with me and you. Doug Rowland has an opportunity to have fellowship with the King of Kings and Lord of Lords. I am somebody special just like Mephibosheth. You have the same opportunity if you have accepted Jesus as your personal Savior.

The Future of Mephibosheth

Once Mephibosheth reached the palace of the king, he ate at the kings table the rest of his life. Can you imagine what a change had occurred in the life of Mephibosheth?

He went from the house of Machir to the palace of the king; from wearing chains of bondage to complete freedom; literally from rags to riches. Look at verse 15, of 2 Samuel chapter 9 (KJV) *"So Mephibosheth dwelt in Jerusalem for he did eat continually at the king's table and was lame on both his feet."* Just because a radical change happened in the life of this young man, this did not change the fact his feet were still lame. When you and I receive Christ as savior, this does not do away with our flesh. We still are in a fleshly body. Remember we have little earth suits that still want its way. And we must contend with the flesh until "the day we get a new body like as unto his glorious body." I have good news for you, our feet will no longer be lame. GLORY !!

Now that we have the story of Mephibosheth completed, we can see how it is much like our own salvation experiences. Let's use those imaginations, to maybe understand, what went thru king David's mind, when he fetched Johnathan's son to the palace. Consider the following:

Let us put David in the place of God the Father.

Let us put Jonathan in the place
of Jesus Christ the Son.
Let us put Ziba in the place of the Holy Spirit.
Let us put Lodebar in the world,
the place of sin we live in.
Let us put Machir in the place of the Devil.
Let us put Mephibosheth in the place of the lost
sinner, lame and in chains at the house of Machir.

I see king David in bed thinking about the days when Jonathan was alive, and the love covenant he made with him. He gets out of bed and walks back and forth in the king's chamber bedroom, wondering if there were any left of Jonathan's family to show them kindness. He summons Ziba to his chambers and asked the question, is there any left of Johnathan's family that I could show my grace to? Ziba bows his head and says yes there is one left of Jonathan's household, his name is Mephibosheth. Well Ziba, the king replies, where does he live and who is he staying with? Once again Ziba bows his head and says O king he lives in Ledebur at the house of Machir. The king exclaims, Lodebar! That place of destitution, that awful valley of no bread, in the house of that old thief Machir! Yes, oh king, Ziba reluctantly states. And even worse, he is lame on both feet, and Machir keeps him all chained up in the back room of that old shack they live in. Immediately king David told Ziba to go and get the white chariot, with the gold star of David on the sides; hitch the five white stallions, go and fetch him out. Ziba does as he was asked and heads for Lodebar. As he is leaving the palace, he looks at the brilliant and vivid colors of the flowers and the big green trees that surround the celestial palace. The further he gets away from the palace, the more gloom starts to set in and as the clouds hide the shine of the son. Ziba knows he is headed to Lodebar. Mud splashes upon the star of David and the stallions get dirt and mud on their white hairs. There were men at the broken-down gate of Lodebar and it stopped the king's chariot. "Where are you going mister ? the men asked. Ziba tells them to get out of the way, he is on business for the king. Ziba yells out Mephibosheth! Then once again he bellows out

Mephibosheth! Machir tries to stop him, but Ziba reminds him he has no power over the edicts of the king. From the very back of the shack, a thin, chain shackled young man comes barely walking to the front porch. I am Mephibosheth, what can I do for you oh Ziba? King David has sent for me to fetch you out of this shack and bring you back to the palace to live out the rest of your days. Loose those chains from him

Ziba demands. Tears began streaming down Mephibosheth's eyes, as Ziba removes the chains and lifts him up and places him in the chariot of grace and mercy. As they leave Lodebar, Ziba tells Mephibosheth the story of the covenant between David the king and his father Jonathan. You mean to tell me I am going to meet the King himself and live and eat at the palace. That is exactly what I am saying Ziba tells him. Mephibosheth says but I am not properly dressed to see the king. Do not worry Ziba responds,he will love you just as you are. Well, GLORY ! On the trip back home, the bushes knock the mud off the chariot and the star of David. And the streams they go through, clean the dirt off of the stallions. Way off in the distance, Mephibosheth looks and says, is that the lights of my new home I see and is that the king waving a banner from the balcony? Ziba answers yes and is also rejoicing knowing what is in store for this young man who was lame on his feet. As the chariot reaches the front entrance of the palace, there is king David. The king was holding brand new garments to place on Mephibosheth 's back and escorts him to the banquet hall. But before they go in, Mephibosheth asked why are you having mercy upon a dead dog as I? The king tells him, I made a covenant with your father that I would take care of you and now you shall eat at my table continually. Does that not give you sort of a picture of salvation, that we believers can compare with ourselves? Thank God for King Jesus. GLORY!

2

IT TAKES A THIEF

1 SAMUEL 30:1-19

Here we are in the books of first and second Samuel again. There so many great stories that have principles for today that happened thousands of years ago. Many well- meaning Christians have the mistaken assumption, that the Old Testament does not need to be read unless it is the book of Psalms . Yet nothing could be further from the truth. We have stories in the Old Testament that open up doors to the New Testament. And we see many lessons that have been penned by the authors that will help us make it thru our Christian life . Whether it be when you are on the mountain or deep in life's valley . Now I want you to know that God wants only the best for you as his child . God wants to see his children prosperous,healthy and successful . I don't mean that in the same way the T.V. evangelist means it. I believe you can be very poor yet still be prosperous . John 10:10 (KJV) says *"The thief cometh not but for to kill, to steal and destroy. I am come that ye might have life and have it more abundantly."* Let's use that one little word 'thief' as we look in 1 Samuel 30:1-19. And please read this as we get into what it may be saying to you. We are aware that our enemies are the world, the flesh and the devil. What we sometimes fail to see is that our open and known enemies can work thru good people and situations that cause you to give way to hard feelings, bitterness, thoughts of revenge, grudges and other emotional feelings. When I used to pastor churches, there was a lady, who up to that point, had been so nice and good to Donna and me. She quit coming for a few Sundays along with her husband. So, one day I dropped in to visit. As soon as I got out of my car, I felt like I should not go in, at least that day. But I went in and said have you been ill the last few weeks? No, she said, we are going to a different church now that you quit speaking to us. I asked her what she meant. She explained she had been going to the mall to shop. On that same day, she said she passed me, and I didn't wave back to her. On that day, I was going home from making hospital visits.

I was headed home from the hospital and did not see her. Evidently, she waved at me when we passed each other, I failed to wave back, and she became angry with me. She then said she had been getting phone calls in a muffled voice asking her to leave the church. Surprise, surprise, surprise as Gomer Pyle would say. Guess who she blamed on making those calls? I knew it was not me. This dear lady had just allowed the devil to use me, to rob her of her joy, peace, victory, love and thinking she had to leave the church she loved. She eventually left her next church all together and never went anywhere. She became a victim of the thief!

Before we get into the meat (main part) of the story in I Samuel, chapter 30, let us briefly look at some things. King David and all the men were out fighting their biggest enemy the Philistines. David had once again gained a great victory. While all the men were gone to fight in the battle, the Amalekites came into their city. They kidnapped all the women and children and burned Ziklag all the way to the ground. When king David returned and saw what was done, he was discouraged. Especially, since his men spoke of stoning him. Let's stop here and bring the next part as we go.

The Party of the Soldiers

The Israelites and the Philistines were always at war with each other and in conflict with each other. In 1 Samuel 30:1 we read king David had left Ziklag to go to battle with the Philistines, one more time. He had great victory, just as he had in the past. If you will recall, it was David as a shepherd boy that defeated the nine foot tall giant with six fingers on each hand and six toes on each foot. The giant was armored from head to toe with solid brass and iron. All David had was a sling and 5 stones: 1 for Goliath, and one for each of his four brothers.

In 1 Samuel 29:5 (ESV) we read *"Is not this David of whom they sing to one- another in dances, Saul has struck down his thousands and David his ten thousands."* Does it not feel good when you by faith in God, see victory over one of your many thoughts and enemies. It is not hard to shout amen and glory when you are on top of the mountain. And I believe that every victory ought to be a time of rejoicing in your life. I also believe that we ought to enjoy those times. Jesus said if we don't rejoice about him the very rocks will cry out.

When I first started going to our present church, when the preacher said something I agreed with, I would open my mouth and say amen or glory. Before long I noticed that others were doing the same. One Sunday a man came to me and said that I needed to stop doing that because it distracted him. He then just said at least think about it. So, I did, for about two seconds, and decided that God was pleased when his people rejoiced over the word, and when spirit anointed songs were sung. So yes, when victories come your way, have your part of praise with Jesus!

The People of Sin

Now then as far as a military maneuver, the Amalekites were shrewd when they saw that there were no men or soldiers, and they overtook the Israelites. They came and stole everything that they had. They kidnapped all of the soldiers' wives and children. After that, they robbed them of everything they held dear to themselves. And if that were not enough, they burned Ziklag to the ground. When we begin to stray from the principles that are laid very plainly in the Bible, we leave ourselves open to our enemies: the world, the flesh and the devil, to come in and rob us of the most valuable things in life. Your joy, your first love, your peace and your testimony. Maybe those precious children may stray into sin, drugs, alcohol, or begin to have sex at an age when they should still be honoring their father and mother. Maybe he will steal the close relationship you at one time enjoyed with a loved one. What has the devil stolen, that was vital to you in your life? Has he stolen that burden you had for souls, and brought them faithfully to God's house? Maybe you used to be active in the choir or men's fellowship time. What about that drive you had for missions or your Sunday School class? Maybe at one time you took time each day with just you and Lord. And somehow, someway, the thief came in and stole those things that at one time you would have fought for. And like a thief in the night, the enemy snuck in and very quietly, slowly, and cunningly, you had some or all of your valuable spiritual things stolen. Things that at one time you held so very important now are gone. If every family that at one time were trailblazers in the house of God came back to church, there would not be room the church to hold them all. But somewhere along the way, someone hurt their feelings, or they felt the pastor said something they did not like . Perhaps they began to slowly allow the thief to cause them to finally quit. In my very first church a man bought a camper. He came to me and said the Lord had given him a camper. Now he blamed that on the Lord. He then said he promised the Lord he would not miss but twelve Sunday's a year. I thought my false teeth would come out, and at that time, I did not even wear dentures. Before we go on, examine yourself and see if the thief has stolen anything that rightfully belongs to you.

Notice verse 6, in I Samuel 30:6 (KJV) *"...but David encouraged himself in the Lord."* I think king David began to recall all the times that God had delivered him from the paw of the lion and the bear while a shepherd boy tending the flocks of his father David. Maybe he thought about all the battles he had won with the people that wished for their doom. Perhaps even defeating the giant Goliath was remembered, knowing it was the hand of God that slew the monster, and delivered Israel that wonderful day. Ever what it was he was thinking, he was encouraged. The next time the enemy knocks you down or just life itself throws a curve ball your way, do as David did. Remember all the times that God rescued you from what looked like sure defeat. Remember how you thought you would never make your bills that one or two times, but God came through just in time. Maybe you got a bad doctor's report, standing somewhere in the shadows, you will find Jesus. Dear reader if you knew the times that things did not seem as if they would work out, and God literally performed a miracle for me, you would call me a liar, liar, pants on fire.

After David encouraged himself in the Lord, we see in 1 Samuel 30:8 (ESV), David began to pray. It was just one sentence *"shall I pursue after this band? shall I overtake them?"* God replied what I am sure David wanted to hear, *"Pursue for you shall surely overtake and shall surely rescue."* In our chapter about prayer, you will find there are times when God will answer immediately. We are creatures that live in the realm of time. God does not live in time. He inhabits time, just as we will, when we are changed in a moment of the twinkling of an eye. For we shall see him as he is.

The Plan of God

God told David you go after them and I promise you will overtake them. Now David went based solely on what God said. He did not have 100 percent of the strength of his men. Remember they said they wanted him to be stoned. There may be times when family, friends and even people that claim to be walking with God may not back you. But if God be for us who can be against us!

Just make jack sure that you are doing what God said through his word and not let your emotions get into it. Your emotions will lie to you. But God will never ever, ever, lie to his children. David asked two simple questions of God and then **waited** on the answer. There are times things go wrong and we just start calling on God, begging and asking and running our mouth. Other times you and I have been so far from God it takes an hour to confess our sins before we can get to God. Do as David did. He asked his questions and then waited until he heard from God. "Psalms 46:10 (ESV) *"Be still and know that I am God I* *will be exalted among the heathen I will be exalted in the earth."* There are times we need to just shut up and listen for God to speak to us through his word. You have to remember that in the Old Testament, God spoke audibly to the prophets. But hath in these days spoke through the word of God, the Bible. David was exercising real faith in what God said to him. Ask yourself this question: When was the last time you did something simply because God said to do it?

The Possession of the Spoils

King David prayed, then he listened to God and relied on nothing, but what God told him to do. He took out after the enemy and recovered what had taken. Read 1 Samuel 39 17-19 (KJV). Two times we read this statement "and David recovered all." What has been stolen from you? Do you have enough faith to pursue what God rightfully gave to you? It does not belong to the world, the flesh or the devil. Go dear reader and pursue. I promise you on the authority of God's word, you shall recover all. GLORY !

The Prayer of David

All the soldiers had got together and blamed king David for what had happened in Ziklag to their families. They even had thoughts of stoning him to death, which came up in their conversation. If I were David, I would be praying also.

3

THINGS YOU DON'T HAVE TO PRAY ABOUT

JEREMIAH 33:3

I guess for every preacher, deacon, teacher, or for that matter, the average saved church member, there are different views about prayer. What is prayer? How long do I need to pray? Where do I need to go to pray? Does prayer really change things? And we could twist the scripture to suit each thought about prayer. Consider the opinions of the following well-known preachers. Johnathan Edwards said I dare not face a day without at least three hours of prayer. But Charles Haddon Spurgeon said in sort of a nutshell, talking to God is not about how long we pray but how sincere we are. D.L. Moody said prayer does two things; it will exercise our faith and establish a relationship with our creator. The great Billy Graham said in the morning prayer opens us up to the mercies and blessing of God. At night it allows us to rest in his hands. There is no doubt, that if we are saved and our prayer life is nearly non-existent, our walk with God will be also. However, there are some things that we need not to even concern God with. There are a few things it is not necessary to pray about. If we know Christ as our savior, prayer is one of our life's blood. Yet after the new birth in Christ there several things we can mark off our prayer list. Matthew's gospel records the very first act of Jesus Christ was his baptism to fulfill all righteousness. In laymen's terms, to be the example for us to follow. Thus, once we are saved, we do not need to ask God the question Do I really need to get baptized? You MUST understand that baptism does NOT in any way save you. If you can't believe me on that, look at the thief on the cross. One bewailed our Savior saying if this man were the Christ, why does he not save himself and us? The other thief simply said remember me when thou cometh to thy kingdom. Jesus replied to that thief, today thou shalt be with me in paradise. There was no time for baptism, for him to be baptized. He would be dead before Jesus said his last words. Again, look at 1 Peter 3:21(KJV)*"The like figure whereunto even baptism doth also now save us."* Now if you stop there you could say that baptism does save us.

But let us read the rest of this verse *"Not the putting away of the filth of the flesh but an answer of good conscience toward God."* Peter explains that the act of baptism does not put away our filth, sin and transgressions, but enables us to be clear with God. Jesus came up out of the water as Prophet, Priest and King hearing the voice of the father This is my beloved son in whom I am well pleased. So, then you can see that you do not need to waste air praying about being immersed in water to signify to the world that Jesus died, was buried and rose again. Another thing that you may mark off your prayer list is taking church communion, more commonly known as the Lords Supper. That is when the grape juice and unleavened bread are partaken. If there is any praying to be done, it should be done before the juice and the bread are passed out. It would be a good idea to read 1 Corinthians11:23-34. Prayer is vital before the service to see if there be any unconfessed sin before taking the Lords Supper. So, we see that this is something you do not need to pray about doing. Praying would be something that is done before church. Another thing we do not have to pray for is to study God's word. There's a reason we need not to pray about studying. 1 Peter 3 : 15 (ESV) *"Always being prepared to make a defense to anyone who ask you for a reason for the hope that is in you yet do it with gentleness and respect."* In order to do this, there is a responsibility to study God's word. That was why Paul wrote to Timothy a command and not a mere suggestion. Paul's instructions are found in 2 Timothy 2:15 (KJV) *"Study to show thyself approved unto God a workman that needeth not to be ashamed rightly dividing the word of truth."* The next thing that does not require prayer is going to church. Now we may need to pray about which church to attend. Always go to a church where Jesus is the center of all attention and the Bible is preached right down the line. In Hebrews 10:25 (KJV) we see God's word tells us *"Forsake not the assembling yourselves together as the manner of some is but exhorting one another and so much the more as ye see the day approaching."* Not only are we to go to church, but we need to go 'so much the more' as we see the Rapture coming. Sadly, statistics tell us that American church attendance is going down about 7 percent. People have stopped going to church for whatever excuse may be given. I am not sure why I just know it is going down. However, it does not change this fact, and I am sure of this fact, that this is a command and not a suggestion that is given in the word, of going and being in the house of God faithfully. Ok grab a hold of your hip pocket and purses because the next one involves the giving of our money to the church . Malachi 3 : 8-11 tells us that we are not to be thieves, but to give to the work of God, in the giving of our money. God even says prove me. In other words, give and see if I do not take care of you. Brethren there have been times my wife and I have given, with not enough money to cover it in the bank. But not one time has a check come back with funds unavailable to make the check good. Dear reader I challenge you to give and see if God does not prove himself to you. Now bring your attention to the new testament, where Paul gives a command, not a mere suggestion, in 1 Corinthians 16 :1 and 2 (KJV) *"Now concerning the collection for the saints as I have given order to the churches of Galatia even so do ye.... upon the first day of the week let everyone of you lay by him in store as God has prospered him that there be no gathering when I come."* Paul gives an order and not a suggestion, to give as God has given unto you. Here is where I have a problem with the Seventh day Adventist. Go ahead and worship on Saturday. However, to give according to what the Bible says, come back to give upon the first day of the week. If John 3:16 is correct, then this text is right also. I am saying very confidently that this is true. God's word from cover to cover is true. 2 Corinthians 9:6-8 tells us that God loves a cheerful giver. But I think he will also take it from a grouch. God wants his church to be givers not just tithers, but as God has purposed. I am serious when I say that God intends for his people to give to the church as God has prospered his people. We need to be in God's house and make sure that it is taken care of financially.

So, we see that God has laid down some things that we do not need to pray about. Prayer is still there for certain things, but not in the areas just covered. They are not good advice, or multiple choice; they are commands by both Paul and God himself. Now then, this does not diminish prayer about all things. Prayer is the link we have to God from all his children. This does not keep us from prayer that keeps our vital fellowship intact. A young man came to my office one day and said I prayed for my girlfriend to come back to me. I advised him with same advice I will be giving to you, as you read this chapter. A few days later that young man took his life because God did answer his prayer. Just not the way he wanted to accept the answer. His mother and father are dear friends of mine. But rather than quit church and blame God, their son's death brought them closer to each other and to God himself. And now over 30 years later they are still living for Jesus. Now then we have talked about the things we don't have to pray about, but there is a flip side. If someone ask me to name the two biggest things a Christian can do, it would be a very speedy answer. First you must be a student of God's word, and second you must be someone who prays. For the few things you don't need to pray about, there are millions of things you ought to be in prayer about. I will use this illustration. Every night my wife and I read out of a book. Right now, we are reading the book "Overcomers" by Dr. David Jeremiah Then we pray together after talking about special requests from one another. One night I thanked God for Coke. Not the snorting kind, the drinking kind. I heard her trying not to burst out laughing. But Coke does not have a more loyal supporter than me. I told her, Donna we are to thank God for everything. Now usually that is the kind of prayer when I talk to him when it's just me and Him. But it sneaked out during our devotions. God gave someone the great knowledge of how to make Coke and because God created everything, he made Coke. And I love them. When we pray, we feel many times like God did not answer prayer. Dear reader you can bank on this statement. God answers every single prayer we pray! Read Luke 18: 1-8 (KJV) A woman had something she thought was wrong and told her story to a judge. She got no satisfaction. She then just kept going and going till finally the judge did give her what she wanted because he said she is bugging me to death. Jesus said in verse 7 of Luke 18, *"And shall not God avenge his own elect which cry day and night unto him though he bear long with them."* The next verse says he would do it *speedily.* Again, in Matthew 7:7 (KJV) Jesus says, *"Ask and it shall be given you seek and ye shall find knock and it shall be opened."* I am not an English major, and you know that by reading my book. However, this is spoken in the linear tense which means keep on asking, keep on seeking, keep on knocking. I am learning that I am to keep on asking Jesus certain things until the answer is clear. Look at James 4:2b and 3 (KJV) *"yet ye have not because ye ask not....Ye ask and receive not because ye ask ye ask amiss that ye may consume it upon your lust."* There are certain ways that God does answer our prayers. Let us look that the ways God answers prayers.

His Answer may be Direct

Remember all those times he said yes to a prayer? O man what a feeling there is when God hears our prayers! David said in Psalms 65:2 (KJV) *"O God thou hearest my prayer."* In Acts chapter12 we find Peter was in jail. I mean he was in a place where he was chained, and 16 soldiers were all around him. Back at the church, they were praying for his release. And what a release it was. God sent power through that place like a bomb had gone off. Peter returned to the church and knocked on the door. A young lady named Rhoda came to answer the door and Peter told her it was him. She would not believe it was him. Basically, she said, it can't be Peter. He is in jail and we are praying that he gets out. Well Duh! God answered the prayer with a great big yes. Look at Joshua 10:12-14. Joshua was in a battle with the Amorites. He prayed Lord I need more time. I need you to help us have enough daylight to finish the battle. God literally stopped time for a whole day. The scriptures say that there has never been a day like this before, or after it, where God heard from a man a request like this. God said yes! A man named Hezekiah asked God to prolong his life and God said yes. And I want you to know, in 2 Kings chapter 20, if you are walking in righteousness, asking with a pure heart, God will say Yes.

His Answer may be Different

After forty-five years of preaching, I have only learned two facts. Fact number one, the Bible is the inerrant word of God without any error or question. Fact number two, there is a God and I and (excuse my Southwest Virginian twang) ain't him. You may pray for something and God answers in a different way than how you prayed. An example of this was a couple that I performed their marriage ceremony. Before they got married, they decided they wanted three children. I can remember the man (I'll call him Blimp), praying out loud "O God I want you to please bless us with three children as soon as possible Lord." You see Blimp's wife was told she would never have any children. That was on January 19th, By October 29th, Blimp was the proud father of triplets. He later jokingly said it was all my fault. We wanted three, but not at one time and so soon! I told him the next time you pray, you had better be more specific. But I am serious, there are times we pray for something and God gives us what we want. But it comes in a different way, from the way we thought it would come. Everyone knows Romans 8:28 (KJV) *"And we know that all things work together for good to those who love God to them who called according to his purpose."* God uses the good and the bad to bring forth something beautiful. Let me illustrate it this way: Everyone who is normal loves chocolate cake. So, what do you say we make one right now? It will be fun so don't stop reading until it is made. First, we need some flour. Now flour by itself is really not part of my food I eat to watch the Panthers play football.

Next, we need eggs. Now eggs are on my menu. I love eggs. So, we dump them into the flour. The next ingredient is vanilla extract. I have never eaten a sandwich and washed it down with that for sure. We will now put in the chocolate. I am a Zero bar and dark chocolate Milky Way kind of a guy. So chocolate is good Next, get a big spoon and dip it in white Crisco. There is not enough money in the world for me to eat a scoop of that stuff. Ok, now let's mix it up and put it in the oven. Hopefully, we will have a chocolate cake ready to eat. I know, I may have left out some things, but you get the point. There may be some rough things in life and some good things in life. Hopefully, it all turns out to be a person, who is a well- balanced Christian.

His Answers may be Delayed

Isaiah 30:18 (ESV) *"therefore the Lord waits to be gracious to you and therefore he exalts himself to show mercy to you. For the lord is a God of justice blessed are all those who wait for him."* I am so glad we have a God that knows us very well. And he knows us from birth to death. We only see now one day at a time. An illustration would be this: we are standing on a porch and the train goes by us. Because of our limitations we are only able to see one car at a time. Not so with Jesus. He is in the heavens and sees the whole train from beginning to end. You pray for a certain thing and God wants us to know, that if the prayer was answered right then, you would do something to mess it up. He says I will answer, but you have to wait a little before you get it, or something else might go wrong. Our text verse for this chapter was Jeremiah 33:3, which tells us that if we call, he will answer. And with that answer, God will reveal things you don't now know. Many years ago, the Happy Goodman Quartet sang a song entitled "The Answers on the Way"

> O yes the answers on the way this I know
> Jesus said it I believe it and it's so
> our heavenly Father knows the need
> before we pray and you can rest
> assured the answers on the way."

It might seem as though you will never get your answer. I promise you there's an answer coming just any day now. *"They that wait on the Lord shall renew their strength."* Isaiah 40:31 (KJV) GLORY!

His Answer may be No

I wish I had the answer for this one. But sadly, I do know the mind of God and neither do you or the TV evangelist. David wanted to build a huge temple to the Lord and God said no. I want your son to build the temple. Jesus does not say no to show us his power. He does not say no to spank us. He says no because he knows the results may bring us further from him, or God can see down the road (remember the train example). A tragedy may occur that would make the family or just one person go through a mess. He is God and I am not. There are times when he says no, and we get mad at God. Don't be that way. Even ask God why if you want to. Jesus sure asked God things while on the cross. "my God, my God, why hast thou forsaken me?" Prayer is an earthly talk to heaven's glories. GLORY!

4

GO AND WASH YOUR GIRDLE

JEREMIAH 13

I attend the Western Avenue Baptist Church in Statesville N.C. My pastor is Dr. Jeff Spry, and he is a wonderful orator and preacher . And if you walked in early you would know who the pastor is . He has on suits that does not draw attention to himself,and his shoes arc always nice and polished . His Grey hair lends an air of dignity to him . But if next Sunday he came to the pulpit wearing a white linen girdle I and about 1,200 other people would say I knew I knew it our pastor has gone and lost his ever- loving mind. And I would say that the majority of other people in other Baptist churches, or for that matter, any church would why are you wearing, question why are you wearing, on top of your clothes, a white linen girdle? If you study very much about the Bible you will find many other strange things that God asked of his prophets, disciple and men of God to do That is exactly what God asked of Jeremiah. For him to put on his loins a white linen girdle and preach to God's people.

When King Nebuchadnezzar took over the Jews, he did not take everyone with him. He took the rich because he could steal all their gold, silver and precious goods and use them for his own kingdom. He then took the middle class because they could build make brick lay stones and other different things that was called skilled labor. But he left the poor behind in that they would be a liability to him to both house and feed. And since God never left his people without a leader or a prophet or a preacher, the prophet Jeremiah was left to the poor ones as a mouthpiece for God. We are going to break down this story of the Old Testament to see what strength we can get from living in New Testament times. Just to lay down some introduction for the story we will look at three things that pop up in my mind.

A Wonderful Sentence or His Call

First, look at Jeremiah 13:1(KJV) "Thus says the Lord to me." Any time that our Lord speaks it is wonderful. Dr. David Jeremiah says that we are so busy talking to God, we never settle back and see what he has to say to us. O I am not speaking of God audibly in a voice we can hear. I mean for a person to stop, be still and allow the Bible to run over us like a nice shower. Psalms 1I9:103 (KJV) "How sweet are thy words unto my taste? Yea sweeter than honey to my mouth." What an awesome thought that the God of the Universe takes the time to desire to have a discussion with me.

A Willing Servant or His Commission

Second, look at Jeremiah 13:2 (ESV "So I bought a loincloth according to the word of the Lord…" Is it not refreshing for God to give a command and God's man does what God requires of him? How willing are we to do what God asks of us? One of my churches I pastored was in Nottingham, Pennsylvania where Dr. Gary Moore is doing such a great work since I left many, many, years ago. A lady that everyone referred to as "Pinky" was married to a man, who later became a good friend. Pinky asked if I would stop by and talk to her husband about the Lord. So, at only twenty-two years of age, full of courage and determination to see her husband saved, I went to see him . Now I did pray that God would melt his heart and rather than listen to God, I prayed and took off . I knocked on the door and Pinky let me in while her husband was on the phone. He was making bets on either horses or dog races . I went into the living room and a baseball game was on the TV. In my heart I was thinking I will today tell the gospel story and he will get saved . When he got off the phone, he said preacher you are welcome in my home, but if you start that Jesus and church stuff, out the door you will go! I sort of laughed inside, but he was a giant of a man . We talked sports for a while .

And then I said to him Ed, I did come here to tell you about Jesus and the gospel . He said Pinky get the door! And with one hand on my collar and one on the back of my belt he threw me out the door. I looked up and next was my Bible flying thru mid- air . I thought to myself . They never covered this in Bible College ! What I failed to do, was after I talked to God, I did not listen to Him talk to me . About one month had past and on a Sunday night while I was in the middle of preaching on the subject "When God sets Your Barley Field on fire", Ed came in the church and ran to the altar and there received Christ as his savior . Later on, he even served on our deacon board. So, it pays to listen to God and do what he tells you to do .

Wicked Society or His Confrontation

In Jeremiah 13:8-11, it would be better for you to turn and read about what Jeremiah was up against. After all Jeremiah had done, the people refused to listen and walked in their own" if it feels good do ways." Dear reader there was a time in my life when Christians were at least respected. Today not only are we disrespected, but we are also laughed at and even blamed for the ills of the world. The main news channels, other than the Fox news, makes "sport" of the beliefs of born- again Christians. Our morals have been set aside by homosexuality, adultery, transgender and living together without being married.

Listen to me dear reader, if it was wrong sixty years ago, it is still wrong today. The Bible states that Jesus is the same yesterday today and forever and thy word is forever settled in heaven. We live in a time of taking the life from even babies that have survived abortion. We murder 300,000 children per year. And I could go on and on about the wickedness of our world. We do not need to hear this so-called prosperity gospel. We need men in the pulpit that with iron throats and

Leather lungs to tell the world that we need a radical change and a world-wide revival. So then with the groundwork laid, let's see why Jeremiah was asked of God to preach to the people with a linen girdle on. What was God trying get the people to do by this funny way? It shows what God wants. The question is, what does God want? Consider the following things.

God wants us Close to Himself

Not only did God ask him to wear the girdle, but he also told him not to wash it. In verse 1of our text it says "and put it not in water. "As much as I love and respect my pastor Dr. Jeff, if he preached Sunday after Sunday and never washed it, that girdle would begin to stink with body odor big time. But in verse 11 of chapter 13, it says "for as the girdle cleaveth to the loins of a man so have I caused to cleave unto me the whole house of Israel." Just to make it plain, God wanted Israel as close to himself as the girdle was to Jeremiah. So many times, in my personal walk with God, and perhaps you too, I will say I want to get closer to God. Well look at your spiritual girdle and see how close you are. I know in a book you should not be repetitious. But again, think about this God. The one who named each star, spoke the world and universe into existence. Made the fish, foul, and animals. Divided land from water. And then took the dust of the earth and rib from the man to breathe into their nostrils the breath of life. And he is still running it all with maybe just a thought, all He created, He wants to be close to little old me. What a theological and spiritual fact that ought to make any of us to shout GLORY !

During the 70's, 80's and 90's I was gone week after week in revivals. One day I was getting ready to leave for NC in a revival after being gone the past ten weeks. At that time, I drove a gray and maroon GMC pick-up truck with a camper top over the back. I put 243,658 miles on that truck. My little girl Jennifer, was about 3 years old at the time, ran and hid in the floorboard and pulled a suitcase over her head. I immediately saw her and asked her what she was doing. She said Daddy you have been gone so much I wanted to go and be close to you. It broke my heart into a thousand pieces. To know she loved me enough to want to be close to me. Well what do you think God feels when his children from the heart say "O God I yearn to be close to you. You see he is always and anywhere you and I are. David says in Psalms 139 7-9 (KJV) "Whither shall I go from thy spirt? Or whither shall I flee from thy presence? If I ascend up into heaven, thou art there: If I make my bed in hell, behold thou are there." Just imagine that kind of love that if you belong to Christ, he will be with you even if you make your life a living disaster, he will never leave you nor forsake you. And the message that Jeremiah was preaching was God wants you as close to him as the girdle Jeremiah was wearing. I must ask this question; are you as close to God as you ought to be? I think in these times we are all living in we could say truthfully, I need to get closer to God with our spiritual girdle. But God does not only want us close to himself, but he also wants to be close to his children as well.

Clean from Hindrances

Now things go a step further. Not only was Jeremiah not to wash the girdle, but God says in verses 5-6 of chapter 13: Take the girdle and go to the river Euphrates, dig a hole in the side of the river and come home. Now this river was several days journey to go. I imagine one of the church members asking where are you going Jeremiah? Down to the river Euphrates. What are you going to do? God told me to go bury this girdle. Can you imagine what was going through their minds? Our pastor is 1 French fry short of a happy meal. But things really took a 180 turn when God the second time said Go and dig up the girdle. Once again where are you going pastor? Going back to the river. What are going to do? Have a resurrection. What are you going to resurrect? Going to resurrect my linen girdle. Then God said to Jeremiah tell the people that you stand for me and that girdle is what they look like in my eyes. Could anything have looked as nasty and stinky as that girdle did? Dear reader what does your girdle look and smell like? God is love incarnate in his son Jesus Christ the righteous, who on the cross took the sin of every man, woman, and child. Past, present, and future, He took it in his body and paid the penalty of sin for the whole world. Just as much as he loves man and his creation, he hates sin passionately, because sin is what hinders us from having a sustained fellowship with our Lord. God really does not ask much from we who are redeemed. One dime out of every dollar, one day a week to get together with other believers, read his word and pray, allow the Holy Spirit to live though us, love our neighbors and ourselves, and to love, worship, adore, honor and obey the Lord Jesus Christ. It is really not too hard to keep a clean girdle. Psalms 51:10 (KJV) says *"create in me a clean heart O God. And renew a right spirit within me… Cast me not away from thy presence and take not thy Holy Spirit within me… Restore unto me the joy of thy salvation and uphold me with thy free spirt."* Psalms 55:22 (KJV) *"Cast thy burden upon the Lord and he shall sustain thee. He shall never suffer the righteous to be moved."* When I feel like my sin starts, my spiritual girdle begins to get dirty, I go to these verses and I claim 1 John 1:9 and I am then clean to fellowship with my Lord. GLORY!

He Wants us Consecrated for Holiness

Brethren when we get close to him, and clean for him, he then can use us to carry out his works. Let us ask ourselves a question. Does our walk back up our talk? Readers, we are in the last days before the Lord raptures the church home, to ever be with the Lord himself. But wouldn't it be simply glorious to see a real, genuine, Holy Spirit lead revival before the Lord comes again? But to see that, we need consecrated Christians that live a life that people can see a in a us difference. Sadly, after all that Jeremiah had done in following what God said to do with girdle, we read the saddest words that could be uttered. Look at Jeremiah 13:11 (KJV) the last five words: *"and they would not hear."* I used to pastor for the first twenty-two years of my forty-five years in the ministry. During that time, I would preach what

I knew would make a difference in the church. No one would move, or change, and it was a most discouraging time. God has a plan for you no matter how young or old you might be. Just remember to every once in a while, take time to see what your spiritual girdle looks like. And if it needs a cleaning, go to the Lord in prayer. Don't do as the Israelites did, they would not hear. Keep your spiritual ears clean and follow God to victory. GLORY !

5

THE DANGER OF BEING GOOD

GENESIS 39:11-23

2 John, verse 8 (KJV) tells us *"Look to yourselves that ye lose not the things ye have wrought (or gained) but that ye receive a full reward."* We only have a brief time on earth to gain rewards that will be placed at the feet of Jesus. And those rewards come from doing good things. Colossians 3:25 (KJV) says *"But he that doeth wrong shall receive for the wrong which he hath done: and there is no respect of persons."* The flip side is the same as doing good, if you do wrong you lose what you may have gained.

Now then, God wants his children to do good, to do good work, do good things and choose good over bad every time we get a chance. Though he still loves us as much as when you do bad, as he does when you do good. His love does not hinge on our performance. But his will is to see good things for us and in us.

Before we can get into how dangerous good works can be, I felt we needed to know why God wants us to do good.

Not Doing Good Brings us Punishment

Hebrews 12:6-11 speaks of chastisement. But he says it is not an act of bad, but good. Any act of God is an act of grace and love. Though while it is happening it may not feel too good. When it is over, it yields peaceable fruit. Peace that you realize afterword may have drawn you closer to the master. Psalms 94:12 (ESV) *"Blessed is the man whom you discipline O Lord and whom you teach out of your law."*

Just as a parent must discipline his children, not because you hate them, but so you can train them to do what is right. You don't have to teach a child to do wrong, you must train them to do good. But when they are disobedient, you must provide discipline. Galatians 6:7 (KJV) *"Be not deceived, God is not mocked. For whatsoever a man soweth that shall he also reap."* The law of sowing and reaping cannot be broken or altered. What you are experiencing now is what you sowed in the past. If you want a bright and prosperous future, then sow good seed now. I think God is grieved when he must discipline his children. As the father of two girls, I had to discipline them. I just know the rare occasions I had to discipline and how it would break my heart into a thousand pieces to spank my little beauties. And yes, I believe in corporal punishment.

Time out worked for me, however how long it took, for me to get out of it. My daddy was a long-haul truck driver and was only home on weekends. He would say boys please be good this week. When I come home, I want things to be happy and not have to spank one of you boys. So, we ought to be good because God does punish if we are not good. But there are better reasons, than that, to do good.

Doing Good will Bring Rewards
While we are still on Earth

Joshua 1:9 (ESV) *"Have not I commanded you Be strong and courageous. Do not be frightened and do not be dismayed, for the Lord you God is with you wherever you go."* God tells us to be good, strong, and courageous; and ever where you go, He will go. In this chapter, they were heading in the direction of the land of milk and honey. God was saying do what's right and while you go, I will be there also. Sadly, they were up and down over this. Matthew 6:33 (KJV) *"Jesus said but seek ye first the kingdom of God and His righteousness and all these things shall be added unto you."* I don't know about you, but I will take all that God wants for me while I am still here. And God says I can have his blessings here on earth if I do good. But there is a better reason.

God Rewards us in Heaven for Doing Good

Did you see what I wrote? We can have things on earth and in heaven just for doing good things. Paul was ready to be killed. Please turn and read for yourself in 2 Timothy 6-8 . There is laid up for me. I say again; there is laid up for me. Laid up in heaven for us to wear the crowns of righteousness. Doing good has so many benefits. How we could even want to stray is a mystery to me. I want something to cast at the feet of Jesus when I get to my eternal home. What about you beloved? But there is a better reason.

Just for the Peace from God for Doing Good

There is a peace that passeth all understanding for just simply doing good. Oh, to experience that peace. You may have to stand alone, the enemy will attack, and you may shed some tears. But there is a peace from God that comes when you decide to choose what is right. One of my favorite songs is "It is Well with My Soul" . When I, thru God's help, have defeated a temptation, peace like a slow-moving river floods my soul. The only way to experience real lasting peace in a world that has no signs of peace, is in Jesus Christ and what he did on the cross. There is a hymn that says: "At the cross, at the cross, where I first saw the light. And the burden of heart trolled away. It was there by faith I received my sight and now I am happy all the day."

It breaks my heart that the old hymns of the faith have been pushed to the back burner. While I love the praise and worship songs, I need a good old fashion hymn every now and then. They carry me back to the time I got saved as an eleven-year-old boy, while attending the church that I would someday pastor for eight years. Dr Gary Moore is pastoring that church and doing a great job. They still sing songs from the green or red back song books. But there is a better reason than that to do good.

Just Because I Love Him and Want to Please Him

My daddy was a long-haul truck driver. Which meant we got to see him from Friday about noon until Sunday evening. When I was eleven and my brother Joe was only eight, the one thing that I knew I could do, was to make sure the yard was mowed, That gave us more time with daddy when he got home. We only had a bad push mower. And our yard was very big, for an eleven-year-old boy. But my two brothers were too young to help, as I said Joe was eight years old and Jeff was only five. But I missed my daddy and wanted to get the yard mowed, because I loved my daddy. I also wanted to please him and spend time with him. At eleven years old my daddy was Superman in my eyes. Daddy won a truck contest by backing into a dock with an egg on top of an orange pylon. He received a plaque that said: " World's Greatest Truck Driver." But daddy could have been a ditch digger and he would still have been a hero to me. That was a great lesson for later on in life as I grew in the Lord. I want to do good because I love him and honor him, for what was accomplished at the cross. When you fall in love with Jesus, then you can move on to a deeper walk with him. You may stumble from time to time and not do good. Confess, repent and get up again walking with him. I want to hear "WELL DONE THOU GOOD AND FAITHFUL SERVANT." Anyone that is a Christian ought to want to do good because they love him and want to please their sweet Savior Jesus.

Now with that in mind, there will be times you will do what's good and right and for some reason you will pay a high price for doing what's good. Notice just a few men who did what was good, but sadly it cost them. Read about men like John Huss who was singing while being burned at the stake. Many other people were tortured. Hebrews

11:34-37 (KJV) gives a good account of what happened to many other heroes of faith. Verse 35 says " ...others were tortured." And while it is true, we ought to do good, there will be times you think you will receive good in return, and it turns out not so good. Just remember Galatians 6:9 (KJV) "And let us not be weary in well doing. For in due season we shall reap if we faint not."

Joseph from Prison to Prince

Potiphar's wife had her eyes on Joseph from the beginning. She asked him to go to her room. When Joseph saw what her plan was, he ran out of there. Now dear reader you may say, why did God not vindicate Joseph? Because God had a bigger plan that even Joseph could not grasp.

Potiphar's wife yelled out rape or whatever word they used in accusations in that day. As Joseph ran away from Potiphar's wife, she grabbed some of his clothing as evidence. He got thrown in prison for a time, but the scriptures say, "But God was with him." Remember his brothers started it all, by throwing him in a pit and he was sold into sort of a slavery. He did good. But doing good placed him in prison. He did not complain, ask why, get mad at God, or even get discouraged. Because of a dream Potiphar had, Joseph was released from jail. Potiphar promoted him to being second in command in the land. Joseph went from a pit to a prison, and God placed him in the position of a prince. God sees what WILL be, we see only what IS at that very moment. Then look at Genesis 50:20 (KJV) "But as for you, ye thought evil against me, but God meant it unto good, to bring to pass as it is this day to save much people alive." God always has a plan for those who want to do what is right and good.

Daniel from the Lions to Laymen

Have you ever watched TV and saw how ferocious are the lions? Not like the one in the Wizard of Oz. I'm talking about those that take pleasure in running animals down much bigger than themselves and making a feast for most every lion in the pride that needs a good feed. In those days they would deliberately let the lions go hungry so they would attack whoever was thrown down in the den. You know it is not even recorded that one lion growled when Daniel was thrown in the den. Eighty years old Daniel was, when he was thrown to the lions. Why, for being good and doing what was right. The King could not even sleep because he was worried about Daniel.

When they let Daniel out of the lions' den, he was in perfect health. God went on to give us an end time picture of the coming of the Lord, along with the revelation of the dreams. Yes, I realize that that God spoke to the prophets in a deeper, audible voice. But in these last days, He has spoken to us through the written word.

The Three Hebrew Children, from Wandering in the Fire to Worshipping the Father

Here we have yet another story that doing good paid off in a hard way. These three Hebrew men had done nothing wrong at all, except not bow down to a heathen idol. The scriptures say the furnace was heated seven times hotter than it ever had before. The only thing that the political pundits could get them on, was failing to worship another god. The three men chose instead to remain faithful to worship the true and living God. But into the hottest fire ever made, the three Hebrew children were thrown. But then, the evil soldiers looked into the furnace and said one to another, did we not throw three men in the fire? They agreed, yes, we threw in three men. I see four walking around, and the fourth is like the son of God. The three Hebrew men came out of the fire. The only things that were burned, were the ropes that had them bound .

What I wanted to get across on this chapter was, that we need to do good. But sometimes doing good does not work like we think. There are times when God has a bigger and better plan for our life. Just do good and allow God to do His work in you. What peace, joy and contentment there is in doing good. God has a plan for you and me!

6

WELL IT WORKS FOR ME, YOU TRY IT

PSALMS 68:19

In Philippians 2:12 (KJV) *"...Work out your own salvation with fear and trembling"* This does not say to work **for** salvation. It says to allow the salvation in you to be personal. That is why my walk with God is exclusive to just me and my Savior the Lord Jesus Christ. There are times when to me he is the King of Kings and Lord of Lords, and I can sing how great thou art, placing God upon his majestic throne. And then there are times when I need a friend to talk to and I can sing what a friend we have in Jesus. Psalm 144:15 (KJV) *"Blessed(happy) are the people whose God is the Lord."* I have a buddy who served as youth director in my second pastorate. He was also called to preach while I was his pastor, whose name is Tracy. One day his wife Sara and my wife Donna traveled to Harper's Ferry. We visited different little get your money stores. In one particular store, Leon Redbone was singing over the speakers a song entitled " I Hate a Man Like You." Now for the past thirty some years, we tell each other, after this shared memory, how much we hate one another. The reason is simple, we laughed our heads off at this song. Until both of us were laughing to tears. I also have a friend at the church I now attend who is not as, let's say, as southern as I am. If I wrote him a note and said I am writing this note because I hate a man like you, it would more than likely not go over as well as it does with Tracy and me.

If you are like me, ever so often life can get a little hard to figure out in an ever-changing world like ours. I am writing this while the COVID-19 virus is making the whole earth do things different. I am one of those who absolutely hate change. I want things to be the same. Change to me upsets my apple cart. I am a Baptist, but that does not tell you much. See there are a lot of different kinds of Baptists. You have Regular, Northern, Southern, Hardshell, Freewill, Missionary and Primitive. I even saw a sign while traveling to a revival at Huntsville, Alabama that said Pentecostal with Visions Baptist Church. Now if that does not make you as confused as a termite in a yo-yo, I don't know what would. Apart from Baptist, there are other denominations Methodist, Presbyterian, Lutheran, Church of God, Church of Christ, Brethren, Mennonite, Adventist and honestly, we could go on and on listing denominations. Understand I am not talking about cultist groups as the Mormons, Jehovah Witness, Branch Davidian, or the Peoples Temple. The last one mentioned saw 911 who drank poison for a false prophet Jim Jones. Then we have sort of ever what you want denomination is fine group, those TV evangelists on a mission to tell you come to Jesus and all your troubles will end and you will be healthy, wealthy and wise. I could write a lot more about that group, but you are more important to me than they are. Along with all the denominations, we have hundreds of Bible commentaries that tell what the Bible is actually saying. I have found if you stick with it, the Bible is its own commentary. Then we have many different versions of the Bible. If you are looking for a version that is different from the standard King James Version, be very careful you do not choose one that changes things like the virgin birth, the perfection of Christ, his sacrificial death and bodily resurrection and his imminent return.

Now then, all these preachers, of all these denominations, using all these versions, want to teach you how to live out your Christian life. And if we are "working out our own salvation with fear and trembling" be very careful you are doing so, based on foundations that have stood the test of time. I understand how people can get a little confused when trying to form your relationship with God, that is both solid Biblically, and seeing him as your King, Lord, Savior, Forgiver, Advocate and Friend.

We are living in a feel- good age. When we go to church, we want to feel good when we leave. What we feel is an emotion and emotions change from minute to minute. As Christians we long for a life full of blessings. Dear reader sometimes God will bless you with a barrel of tribulation to teach us patience. Why? Because the word teaches "tribulations worketh patience." Be very careful what you ask for, you just might get it. This is why I do not like to be labeled as religious. Call me a Christian, a believer, saved, or born-again. Religion will send you down a road of disobedience. True relationships with Christ will bring you victory. Now then, I am speaking to those of you who really want the joy of feeling victory in your life, no matter what denomination or what version of the Bible you use. It works for me, try it, if it doesn't work for you, then find a way that does. I have been in the ministry forty-five years and I have been saved fifty-three years. It has just been in the last three or four years, that I began to know God and how can I feel victor. Look, all of us are living in what Dr. Bill Guillum called an earth suit. That refers to the fact that we are in the flesh. In a fleshly body, we must deal with a warfare of flesh against the spirit that lives in you, in the person of the Holy Spirit. Turn in your Bible and read Romans 7:15-25 and you will see what I mean.

Now then every denomination has what they call Truth, Works, Feel and Faith. We all have three basic enemies; the world, the flesh and the Devil or Satan or ole' slew foot. Let's sort of use our imaginations and think of things like this. The world is a patch of woods that we go into everyday of our life. The Devil according to 1 Peter 5:8 is as a roaring lion, that walketh about seeking whom he may devour. So, this lion, is running through the woods of the world, wanting to devour you and me both. But in those woods, there is a log cabin. It is built with huge logs, snuggled together, with rock hard cement keeping it together. The logs are at least two feet in diameter and the roof is likewise built to a point with solid logs. It has one door that pulls open from the inside. Four smaller logs fit across the door into slots. It has four bolt locks on it and six heavy chain locks. And for good measure, a chair fitted up against the doorknob. Now then, if you are talking about safe, that cabin is tighter than Fort Knox. This cabin represents none other than our Lord Jesus Christ himself. You get up every day to go to work or school or wherever you choose to go. Things are going great, when out of the blue, here comes the lion thru the woods and has you in his sights. Well for one thing you don't just stand there like a dooffus. If you have any sense at all, you are going to make a bee line for the cabin. You get to the cabin, shut the door, place the four logs on the door, put the chains in their place and lock all the bolt locks. Now I have a question. Are you safe? Truth is yes, you are safe from the paws and jaws of the lion. Why are you safe? The cabin can't be penetrated. The cabin represents truth, it represents Jesus, he is the way, the truth, and the life (John 14:6). Notice four things that helped me work out my own salvation.

The Cabin is Truth. I am Safe

In the spiritual world, yes, I am safe. I am in the cabin and since it represents Jesus, whether I feel safe or not, I am safe. Truth should override feelings when we are in truth, but because I am in the flesh my flesh is still scared. Even in the midst of truth, our flesh really tries to throw all its power onto our little earth suit that it can handle. When Jesus died at Calvary and shed his blood, then the third day rose again, Jesus defeated death, hell, the grave, sin, and best of all Satan was defeated when he was thrown out of heaven. But he was crushed when the blood was shed, and the body of Christ physically came out of the grave. That ought to make a Quaker shout amen! You see Jesus is the living cabin. If you were to turn and read Hebrews chapter 11, you would get a partial list of people who had dealings with the lion, Satan, or our Enemy. Base your life, family, church, job, and your unique walk with God on truth. Truth cannot be altered, in that truth is totally fact based. Spiritually speaking truth is a person not an idea.

Jesus was not an idea thought up by some wayward political zealots. Jesus told them in the upper room at the last supper, I am the WAY, the TRUTH and the LIFE. So, if truth is a person when the enemy comes, I stop him not with rhetoric from the brain of a dead prophet. I can stop him through the power of Christ, who is the living word.

Next is Faith. I Believe I am Safe

Next, because I am in the cabin, I believe I am safe. Truth must be the object of my faith. Since Jesus is the *living* cabin, the object of my faith is Jesus Christ. I am inside an impenetrable person/object. Yes, there are times when I falter and fail. And I have devoted a whole chapter on this. But for now, please understand there will be times you forget how safe you are in Jesus. The disciples said to Jesus *"Lord I believe, help thou mine unbelief."* Jesus said if we have faith of the grain of mustard you can say to the mountain be thou removed, and it will be removed. You may have enough doubt to sink the Titanic, but just a little faith moves the mountains in your life. When you are in Christ the results are that faith is activated and will produce works. Once a person receives Christ as savior, faith is the act that produced in you your salvation. Think about salvation for a second . Salvation is a work of faith. When we take Jesus as savior, we are trusting a person to take us to heaven and keep us from hell for eternity. Now if God's son is great enough to do that, then anything else in life should be faith based. I am in the cabin that is truth. The lion cannot penetrate this cabin because the cabin is stronger than whatever is outside. Whether a lion, bear, rain, snow, windstorms, trial, temptation, and we could go on and on. Once you are in the cabin you are safe. And you can believe you are safe because of the solid build of the cabin. Understanding that the cabin is Jesus, God's ONLY begotten son. Just imagine how safe we are being in him. The very nature of God is in me, in the person of the Holy Spirit. We might hear the lion roar and scratch. But he does not have a chance at getting in!

The Next Step is Works. I Can Act Safe

Truth is I am safe from the lion. Jesus is the living cabin. Next is faith that the lion could not get in, so I can believe I am safe. Now then since I am safe, I believe I am safe. I now can act like I am safe. I can read, I can pray, I can tell the world the gospel story. The lion can roar, scratch, jump up and down, do anything he wants. But I am in the living cabin Jesus, so I can do works that prove my faith is real. James said faith without works is dead. I do not want a dead faith. I want a faith that lets Jesus know my faith is in him and him alone . I guess the question of the hour is are we as Christians knowing what we know are we acting on our faith . James declares that faith without works is a dead faith . Real, true, and genuine faith will produce not just works but also fruit. Now, follow me. Fruit and works are two different things. Yes, works prove faith, fruit had to grow, and the longer you learn of Christ, the more the fruit will grow in you. This is called progressive sanctification. The Holy Spirit is a person. The more we yield to him, the more He will live through us! Sadly, many people claim to be a Christian, but their lifestyle does not back up Christianity. But you and I are not going to be in that number. Well if we are not going to be in that number, faith must have a working faith.

Lastly Comes Feelings. I Now Feel Safe.

I was raised a Baptist and I am still in the Baptist denomination. I feel like I can say that most Baptists want feelings first, then go to the rest of the steps. I can shout Glory, Amen, Praise the Lord, because the object of my faith is rooted in truth and the object of my faith realizes how powerful is my living in the cabin. Dear reader he has everything under control. At times things may not go as I would hope they would, but because He lives, I can face any day, or anything that comes while I am out in the woods. Most people want to do this in reverse. We want feelings first and that is not God's divine plan. Don't be a pouter be a shouter. Allow yourself to be one that feels safe in the arms of God. Well what I have given to you in this short chapter works for me. Try it you may like it!

---7---

THE DEATH OF A BRILLIANT FOOL

2 SAMUEL 3:31-39

Outside of the rapture of the church, there is an appointment that every man, woman and child will face and that is the appointment of death. *Hebrews 9:27 (KJV) says "And as it is appointed unto men once to die, but after this the judgement."* There is no getting around this appointment . You can't call it off, change the way, or manner of how it comes. Of all the mysteries that there are in this world, death is the biggest mystery. Now I have my own personal opinions of what is called near death experiences and that is a very controversial issue. But the death of Abner is really unique in that King David says in verse 33 of 2 Samuel, chapter 3, Abner died as a fool. Then King David says that he was a great man in verse 38 of that same chapter. So, what is the answer? The answer is, he was both just like 95 percent of all people. Now you can in this life be smart, brilliant, successful and strong. But if you do not trust in Christ as your Savior, you will be a brilliant fool at the moment of death. Dear reader this time we have on earth is so very temporal. But this life is just a preparation time for an eternal existence. This story is so very relevant for today. Paul says if this time on earth was all there was to it, then when we die and it is all over with, we would be miserable. So, you and I together will look at the events that happened in the life of Abner for King David to make such a statement.

There are several people involved in this great story: Joab and his two brothers Abishai and Asahel. Then Abner and of course King David himself. So, let us get started with Abner being the center of attention.

His Fearful Danger

Abner was one of the greatest soldiers there was in the army of King David. There were likely men under him that he was in charge of. One of them was a young man named Asahel. Remember that he had two brothers Joab and Abishai. Jealousy got in Asahel heart and desired to have Abner's rank and power. So, the only way to do that was to kill Abner. He began to follow Abner everywhere he went to get a chance to kill him. Abner finally offered a compromise with Asahel. He told him, you choose which way to go and I will go the other way. Asahel would not hear of it and it all came to a one on one, old fashioned fight. Abner took his spear and with the blunt end of it, thrust it in Asahel's chest. In second Samuel 2:18-24 you can read all about it. Abner either kills Asahel or gets killed himself. Now Abner has a problem. In those days there was what was called an avenger of blood. Which meant that Asahel's two brothers had a right to seek out the one that killed a family member. They could kill the one who murdered that sibling. Abner had a problem, rather than try to deal with one, there were two after him.

May I say at this at this time, that we are strangers of this world if we are saved by the grace of God. The Bible says that Satan is the god of this world and being saved he is out to kill us. Only God himself is all powerful. Yet you and I are his enemy because we are children of the one who booted him out of heaven. He was thrown out of heaven because of his pride and arrogance. That's why the scripture declares pride cometh before a fall. John 10:10 (KJV) declares 'the thief cometh not but to steal and to kill and destroy…" . Notice that he wants to KILL you and me. We are in a state of danger in this world. As an illustration, consider this example. My little girl, Laura Beth, walked with me to the mailbox one day. As we walked, a semi-truck came down the road. She grabbed my leg tight and I asked her what was wrong. She was scared thinking the truck was going to hit us. The sun caused the truck to cast a shadow. I told her that it was only the shadow. I got to thinking that the devil wants to kill us but *"Yea though I walk through the* valley *of the shadow of death I will fear no evil for thou art with me thy rod and thy staff they comfort me ."Psalms 23:4 (KJV).* When Jesus died on the cruel cross of Calvary he got hit directly with the truck of death . God's children only have the shadow. If that does not start a fire in your heart, then your wood is wet. GLORY! But be alert of old slew foot, he wants us dead. Do you have a friend that is going to hell? Do you have a family member that is lost without God? Brothers and sisters, I plead with you and even beg of you, do all you can to get them to Jesus. Hell is real, literal, eternal, and true. And people who reject God's son go there. Beloved when was the last time you heard an entire message on hell?

His Foolish Death

God always has the answer to death . Our Lord set up six cities that you can run to for refuge for the avengers of blood. And when you get there, a priest would look at the evidence and determine guilt or innocence. These 6 cities were Golon, Ramoth, Shechen, Hebron, Kedesh and Bosor . You may have killed someone through an accident of any kind. You could go to one of these cities. Perhaps it was first degree murder, you just flat out killed a person for personal reasons. Then you could go to the cities of refuge or go on the lam. Maybe it was self-defense, as in the story of Abner taking the life of Asahel. Your only relief from the avengers of blood was getting to one of the cities. How foolish it is for someone to die and go to hell. Dear reader I put this chapter in for several reasons. One was in hope someone lost, without God in their life, would somehow read this book and get saved. Another reason is, that someone saved would get someone lost on your heart and do all that is possible to see them give their heart to the Lord. The reality of heaven and hell ought to be one of the top things on your prayer list .Who do you know that has never been saved? Abner knew where all the cities were located. In fact, everyone knew where the cities of refuge were located. So, he knew, yet did not go. I did an experiment for two days about two years ago. I watched Christian TV for forty-eight hours. I stayed awake literally two days. And in forty- eight hours I did not hear the word hell mentioned one time. In forty- eight hours I never heard the simple plan of salvation mentioned. I did hear "Seed and harvest giving" . I even saw with my eyes and heard with my ears to send for miracle spring water. I was in shock to hear a man tell people if you read certain scriptures, pray a certain prayer, open this plastic spoon full of water and they would be healed and have more money than you can spend! If that's not bad enough it gets worse. Because people were actually sending in with "love gifts." Sane men and women were giving to men, who are nothing more than legalized extortionists . Two days that I could have been fishing, hunting, or playing golf went down the drain. We need so desperately a real, genuine, 100 percent move of Christians following God's word. Abner was a great warrior and soldier, but his death was very foolish.

His Friendly Deception

Joab and his brother Abishai finally catch up with Abner in Hebron. Look at 2 Samuel 3:27 (KJV) " And when Abner was returned to Hebron, Joab took him aside in the gate to speak with him quietly and smote him there under the fifth rib that he died for the blood of Asahel his brother." Can you imagine with me what is said here? Not only was he at Hebron, but he was also at the gate. Joab knew if Abner took just one step inside the gate, he would not be able to avenge his brother's death. Notice the word quietly. Joab used some sort of deception to get Abner to take one step out of the gate of Hebron, took his spear or some implement of death, stabbed him under his fifth rib and a great man fell to the ground and died. Precious reader mark my word that the devil will do whatever is necessary to keep people from getting born-again. Let me show you how close a sinner is to getting saved. Romans 10:8 *"...the word is nigh thee even in thy mouth and in thy heart..."* In the old testament one step for refuge. In the new testament a person is one word away from eternal life with the King of Kings and Lord of Lord. Because if you say the first word, the rest will follow, and Jesus saves from the gutter most to the uttermost. There is no limit to the love of Jesus. A preacher friend of mine was talking about the love of God in a way that really got to me . I am a WW II buff. I like reading about and watching documentaries on WW II. Adolf Hitler was maniacal for the murder of more than six million men, women, and children. Beloved he said if Hitler himself came to repentance, that Jesus' blood would save him. I was very young in the ministry and when I finally realized what was the depth of God's love. Then I flipped to the page of the one who is second in power. I then realized that Satan will, deceive as hard as he can, to keep a sinner from Christ and Christians from a close walk with Jesus.

Listen closely to this, the Holy Spirit is to us, what Jesus was to his disciples . And the devil does not care one bit what he needs to do to get his job done. Abner could have said you need to talk to me, come over here. But he did not, and it cost him his very life. How many Abners do you know? What are you going to do about it?

His Final Determination

Dear reader in closing, this chapter I really want you to allow the Holy Spirit to speak to you. No one, and I mean not one single person, ever can grasp with our minds what eternity is. I have been preaching since I was seventeen years old, and I stopped years ago trying to give an explanation of eternity. Let just an old Southwestern Virginian give you a definition of eternity. Are you ready? OK, here goes "It's a long time". When Abner's body hit the ground, it was the last time he had to change his mind. When you die there not an oop's I need more time. There are two roads to travel on: The narrow road and the broad road. There are two foundations to build your life on: the rock or the sand.

There are two places for eternity: heaven and hell. And there are two powers: power of a defeated Lucifer and the power of God Almighty. All of life is made upon choices. Abner was a good man, good leader, great soldier. No doubt Abner's name was really known. However, this story is a story of the death of a brilliant fool!

8

THERE'S NOT MUCH SHADE UNDER THE JUNIPER TREE

I KINGS CHAPTERS 17-19

In the prophet Elijah we see sort of the way things go for those of us that are saved. There are days, weeks, even months, when things seem to go well and about everything you do is victorious. Then from out of the blue, things just seem to fall apart.

Do not listen to the "joy boys " on TV. I believe that God allows certain trial and heartaches. Maybe things do not seem to go your way. The "joy boys" will tell you come to Jesus and everything will be great. You will have plenty of money and plenty of good things will happen and your health will be perfect. Just keep sending *that* seed faith money or drink the miracle water. Beloved these men are deceiving people by the multitudes. Men and women and even smaller children have fallen prey. They live like a movie star and have more money than you can possibly image. And what breaks my heart is to see older ride this money train, with many cutting down in food and needed medicine, just to send these guys money. If you want God to really bless you, give your money to the local church you attend. As long as it is a Bible preaching conservative church. We do not have much time left, so in these last days, let it be days of walking with the Savior consistently. We have enough yo-yo Christians, that are up and shouting one day, and down and pouting the next day. The Bible says Jesus Christ, the same yesterday, today and forever more. We are not Jesus, but we can set a goal to follow his example. Elijah was a great man, but even great men will blow it from time to time. Let us get into this story of a great, great, man who possibly will come back as one of the two witnesses during the tribulation period, to proclaim God's word.

The Message from the Prophet

The word of the Lord came and told Elijah there shall be no dew from the ground, nor rain from the sky, unless at his very word. However, he told Elijah to go to the brook Cherith and he would have water and the ravens, one of the dirtiest birds there are, would bring him meat. Beloved this is a very important event to keep in the back of your mind as we go. I don't think I would be out of line by saying there is a famine in our land over the preaching the gospel. We have plenty of preaching about how to gain money, get wealth, and stay healthy. But the message of the cross must be the preeminent message to people. Dear reader the cross is the very hub of our Christianity. *1 Corinthians 2:2 (KJV) "For I am determined not to know anything among you save Christ and him crucified."* Paul wanted this church at Corinth to know that the very basic message that needs to be preached is the death, burial, and resurrection of God's son, the Lord Jesus Christ. There is nothing wrong with riches and good health. However, reader all of that is a result of what was completed on Mount Calvary when Jesus dipped his life into death, to give to you and me the great blessings, that come along with being born again. When I began preaching forty-five years ago, I was told by Dr. Bill Stafford, never preach, not one message, that you do not mention the cross upon which Jesus died. Preaching the cross will accomplish the following five areas in our lives.

Sheds Light on our Sin

You will never be able to get saved until first you see yourself as lost, without hope in this life or the afterlife. When Adam fell (sinned) it put all mankind under sin. We are sinners by nature, by practice, and by choice.

Satisfies God's Mandate

The very last thing that Jesus said as he was raised into the heavens, was for we that are born into his family, to GO to all the world and proclaim the gospel.

Saves Those That are Lost

There is no other name that can save a person from hell except the message of the cross. The word says *even so faith cometh by hearing and hearing by the word of God*. Not wealth, or wisdom, not because your parents were saved, not being baptized or even going to church can save you. You are saved through the power of the cross and the death, burial and resurrection of Jesus. That is your only hope, the cross of Jesus.

Strengthens our Faith

The gospel of Jesus ought to be the anchor of your soul. At the foot of the cross is all the strength you need to face whatever your enemies may throw at you. And let me say, when you do get born-again, you will face enemies that are slick, tricky, and devious.

Continuing with the story of Elijah, consider a problem he faced.

Maiden with a Problem

The brook at Cherith dried up and God told Elijah to go to the widow Zarephath's house and God would sustain him there. When he got to the widow's house, he found she had many problems. She only had enough meal and a little oil, that she was going to use to make them one last meal. Then they would die, no doubt from starvation, because her husband was dead. Elijah told her that she was to fix for him first and from that time on, she would be well fed. The oil and meal would never run out. While he was there her son was in a loft and had died. Elijah stretched himself three times over the body of the boy and he was revived. Just as I reminded you to remember the brook, please put this story in the back of your mind. In the book of Matthew 6:33(KJV) we read *"but seek ye first the kingdom of God and his kingdom and all these other things shall be added unto you."* And may I interject that if you and I will place Jesus first, we will have what he wants us to have, even the desires of our heart. Because if you are putting him first, your desires will be in line with God and the eternal, not the flesh. The problems of the widow were all taken care of for the rest of their days. David said, *"I have never seen the righteous forsaken nor his seed begging bread."* (Psalms 37:25 KJV) I will add that there was a time after I broke my back, when money was very, very, tight for us. And I mean tight. There were times when we did not have money to spare for anything. I could not preach because I was in a back brace and could not stand. All we had was Donna's income. We picked out a house to rent from a man. Before we moved into the house, he said we could rent it for eight hundred dollars a month. While a good deal, it was still a stretch. But when we moved, he denied saying eight hundred, and that it would be 1400.00 dollars per month. We began to tithe, and God blessed even more. Yes, it was hard, really hard. But when all was said and done, we never missed a meal, buying clothes, or anything like that. You simply have to place God first and we did.

Next, we will look at Elijah in his time of the trial of his faith. He had a time of victory and a time of defeat. First, we will see his victory.

The Marathon of Prayers

Now we have a couple of more names in this story. There was Elijah, Ahab and his ungodly wife Jezebel in chapters 18 and 19. Now the God of Ahab and Jezebel was a god named Baal. And they instructed all the people of the land to fall down worship the god Baal. Here comes the prophet Elijah that served the true and living God, the great I am. There was a challenge made about who was the right and true God. Do you have any place, anything, or any person you place before the living God? Then you are as bad, if not as bad as,

Ahab and Jezebel. It's good to take inventory of our priorities. Just ask yourself this question, do I really have my priorities as a Christian where they ought to be? So, things were all set upon Mount Carmel. The worshipers of Baal prayed and prayed, that Baal would answer their prayers. Soon it was noon and Elijah began to make fun of those who were praying for Baal to answer. In 1 Kings 18:27 he said cry louder! Maybe he is talking to someone or pursuing after something. I know, he is on a trip and is not at home or maybe he is taking a nap. He laughed at them until they began to cut themselves with lancets and knives. The Bible says they did this until the blood begin to flow. They prayed till the evening and then it was Elijah's turn. Elijah took twelve stones in a circle, one for each tribe of Jacob. He then dug a trench around the bullock and wood in the middle. He then took twelve barrels of water and poured over the sacrifice. Then Elijah said a sixty-three word prayer and the fire fell from heaven, consumed the sacrifice and licked up the water. That deserves a great big AMEN! Then in 1 Kings 18:41 the rain fell in abundance. Can you imagine how on top of the mountain Elijah must have felt to watch the embers of coals that fell down on the sacrifice? Think back, you that have been saved, at all the times God answered some big prayers for you. Maybe a special church service that meant more to you than most. That sick child that got well, that heart attack that you or a loved made it through. Maybe cancer that went into remission. Time after time, God came through, true to his word, as he said he would. Those are special times in all of our lives.

We will now look at Elijah's time of defeat.

The Mood of the Perverted

Word gets back to an old wicked, perverted woman from a hen-pecked husband Ahab, of what had happened on Mt. Carmel. In short, she said you go tell that prophet by tomorrow about this time, I will have his head. Now Elijah had just the day before prayed down fire from God. Now this old witch has threatened to kill the prophet. And rather than trust in God he ran like a rabbit. Now do not be too hard on Elijah when you have not walked in his sandals. 1Kings 19:3 (KJV) says "when he saw that" what she was going to do, he saw himself dead, and made a very hasty run into the wilderness. He ran to Beer-sheba where Judah, his servant remained. Then Elijah ran another day's journey into the wilderness. His choice in what to do was from fear and he had run. Take some good sound advice from an old man like me. Never make a decision when you are down in the valley, or up on the mountain top. Always make a decision when your emotions are at a good level place in your heart and mind. Hasty choices almost never are the best choices to make and almost never reflect God's help with your decision. Take time to weigh all your options and make a good Jesus led choice.

Remember I had instructed you to keep the brook Cherith in the back of your mind? Now we see Elijah when his life "fell apart."

The Misery of the Preacher

This old preacher, Elijah, to me had some sort of a nervous and physical break down. And in complete exhaustion, he landed under a Juniper tree. There's not much shade under these trees. But he was worn out mentally, emotionally and physically. Have you ever been in that spot? A few years ago, while still trying to pastor a good- sized church, I preached four months straight, every night in revivals, and two times on Sunday. When I did get a break, I did not care if I ever preached again. I could not do anything for my family. And I felt like the whole world was against me. I knew I was not in a place of fellowship with God. I called a preacher friend of mine and told him how I was feeling. He said call someone to preach Sunday morning. Take a hot shower, just as hot as you could stand it. Stay in it a least thirty minutes and then go to bed. I did what he said and slept ten hours. He said when you get up, eat you a good meal and go back to bed. I did and slept twelve hours. I took the week off and spent time with my small children and my wonderful wife. I went back to bed and slept eight more hours. I woke up and ate again and things began to be OK again. I was completely exhausted and needed to withdraw myself until I could pull myself back together. The preacher that gave me that advice had gone through the same thing before me. Now this precious friend is with the Lord.

Elijah went through a similar thing. Totally exhausted the Lord sent an angel to minister to him. Remember I told you to remember the water at the brook, the cake of food at the widow's house, and then the Mount Carmel fire that fell. Notice what the angel did.

Showed Him a Cruse of Water

I would be willing to bet he remembered how God provided him water at the brook Cherith. A drought everywhere. But where God told him to go to the brook there was plenty of water. God was reminding him of his care for him.

Showed Him the Coals

Don't you imagine his mind drifted back to Mount Carmel. He remembered how God answered a sixty-three little word prayer and brought the fire down from the heavens. He laughed at the prophets of Baal, and God consumed the alter and drank up the waster he poured out. Dear reader there are going to be . days when you can feel like you could pull down the fire. But there will also be days when you find yourself under a Juniper tree God will love and take care of you no matter where you are. Remember *Psalms 139:7-9 (KJV) "Whither shall I go from thy spirit ?or whither shall I flee from thy presence if I ascend up in to heaven thou art there if I make my bed in hell behold thou art there if I take the wings of the morning and dwell in the uttermost parts of the sea even there shall thy hand lead me and thy right hand shall hold me."*

9

YOU ARE NOT THE ONLY ONE TO BLOW IT

PSALMS 78

Rather than take up space in this book, get you a Bible out and read carefully and slowly in the book of Psalms 78:37-39 . We will be looking at other scripture in this chapter and others as we go. Proverbs 15:13 (ESV) says *"A glad heart makes a cheerful face."* Proverbs 17:22 (ESV) says *"A joyful heart is good medicine."* Would it not be a blessing if every day when you woke up you heard the birds singing, the sun was shining, the coffee was perfect, and **you were in perfect harmony with our Lord**? However, there are days when you are trying to walk with God, and you are doing your best to keep in fellowship, but before you know it, you have blown it. Sometimes it's a hand grenade, and sometimes it's a nuclear missile. Chapter 78 of Psalms shows us two things. Number one, it shows us the damage of man's failure. Number two, it shows us the depth of God's forgiveness. I am so thankful for Psalms 78:39(KJV) *"For he remembered they were but flesh…"* Now then you too, dear reader, ought to be very thankful for this verse. What if God demanded perfection after you received Christ as Savior ? Most of us would be dead before the night of getting born again. I am saying a great big GLORY that he remembers I am just made of sinful flesh. He knows his children because of the fall of Adam has a continual battle between the flesh and the spirit . Over and over and over again, God's people would worship him, walk with him and commune with him. Only to turn and have nothing to do with the God that brought them out of the house of bondage. I have heard it said if God and Moses ever agreed at o the same time about God's people, they would have been killed off. One minute, Moses would say kill them all God. They are a stiff neck bunch that will never obey you . God would reply and say I love them Moses and they will come around. Then God would say tell them to prepare to die I am weary of their sins and transgressions. Moses would say no, God I think they will pull themselves up and worship you once again. This sounds a little humorous but if you read the first five books of the Bible, you will see the arguments that God had with his prophet. It just seemed like Israel was on a roller coaster ride spiritually. Does that not remind you of we Christians that are walking with him one day, or week, or month. And then we do something that causes us to think we have blown it. Then most of the time we quit altogether. I say again if all the people that used to be faithful to church came back, we would see a world - wide revival. There would not be enough room to accommodate everyone. I go to the best church in the United States of America. Everyone should think that about their church too. We have a big church and must have two services. I go to the 8:30 am service and we have about 460 people. Then in between first service and second service, we have Sunday School. he second 11:00 am service has about 660 so on average, and we have between 1100 and 1200 total. But on Easter last year we had 1864. And there was more who at one time were faithful. And as the children of Israel, those Christians have now quit. If you are one of those please get back to serving God . If you have truly been born-again you have to be living a miserable life . Because Jesus is the way the truth and the life . And if you are saved you can't be happy without Jesus in your life. Do not wait one second longer to get right with God and get into a good Bible preaching church. My oldest daughter, who lives in Montana now, entered a foot race when she was in elementary school. When she was born, she was a late comer, and her foot was turned just a bit. But the doctor said she e would grow out of it which she did. There was a crowd of children there, but my eye was not on anyone but my daughter. They blew the whistle and off they went. She was not in first place, but she was up front. But all of a sudden, her shoe came off and my heart broke. As they say, God squeezed my heart and juice ran out my eyes. But she did not quit . She sat down put her shoe back on and ran the rest of the race. And guess what? She came in first place? No, she was last in the race. But she was first in my heart. I knew then that she was going to be a person that would never quit. She was valedictorian of her class and wanted to be a CPA. Most people take two or three times to pass the CPA examine. But not her. She passed the first time. Her first job was with Price Waterhouse Cooper in Boston, Massachusetts. What is so funny we thought this brilliant young lady would be in the business world and make tons of money. She now lives on a small farm with her husband, who is a fine Christian. I am blessed with five grandchildren. Now how was that for a doting man full of pride for his children. I said all that to tell you, there are times as we run the race of life, that we all run when our shoe is going to come off and we think we have blown it. Well la-DE-da you are a chicken. Quit feeling sorry for yourself and get back up again. Remember what is written in Proverbs 24:16 (KJV) "For a just man falleth seven times and riseth up again."

Now then, before we go any further in this chapter, I do not want you to think that it is OK to sin. The attitude of "oh well I can live anyway I want to, and God will look over it and forgive me" is not correct. This was the sort of attitude of some of the Romans. But listen to what Paul wrote to them in Romans 6 :1-2: (KJV) *"What shall we say then shall we continue in sin that grace may abound? God forbid. How shall we that are dead to sin live any longer therein?"* God hates sin. I know you have heard this a thousand times, but while God hates sin, he passionately loves his children. He hates sin because sin is what nailed his son to the cross. Sin is what separates his children from himself. And it grieves the heart of God when we sin. Proverbs 14:9 (KJV) "

Fools mock at sin." Proverbs 14:34 (KJV) *"But sin is a reproach to any people."* This chapter in no way should glorify sin or to make sin seem, for lack of a better word, *normal* for the ones who are saved.

However, there are going to be times when we do just mess up royally. I feel so ashamed of the times I have let my precious Savior down. As hard as you try, there will be times when you really do get wounded in the warfare of Christianity. Understand I am not religious, I am a child of the King. I am in a warfare not of flesh and blood, but principalities, and spiritual wickedness in high places. The devil shoots fiery darts at us and every so often, we will get hit by the darts. I believe on the Judgment Seat of Christ most Christians will in sorts be limping to the victors stand. Also understand that every single person, no matter who you are, has faced the same things you are also facing. Look at I Corinthians 10:12 and 13 (ESV) *"Therefore let anyone who thinks he stands take heed lest he fall. No temptation has overtaken you that is not common to man. God is faithful and he will not let you be tempted beyond your ability, but with the temptation he will provide the way of escape, that you may be able to endure it."* Even our Lord and Savior was tempted in the wilderness. Luke chapter 4 gives this account. Notice that he did not tempt him until he had fasted forty days. Satan waited until Jesus the man, was at his weakest before he tempted him. And if you think about it, most of the times we blow it, we are at our weakest point and he hits us with temptation. You are not alone when you blow. It doesn't matter who you are, or what you have done. Let us break this down in outline form hoping you can remember it a little better

1.All Have the Same Forgiveness

If you will read 1 C0rinthians 6:9-11 you will read a list of wicked sins. Here Paul made a list of sins, that at one time, these people were involved in adultery, homosexuality, thieves, drunkards, swindlers, liars and more. Paul says at one time you were involved in these sins, but now you are clean.

It does not matter what you did before you Got saved that, is thrown in the sea of forgetfulness and a "NO FISHING" sign put up. GLORY!

Why do you think that God will forgive you of the sins you did before you got saved and then stop his forgiving you after you are saved? When Christ died and shed his blood, it was forgiveness of all sins that were past, present and future. We are going to find out that some of the greatest people in the Bible, had times when yes, they blew it too. And I don't mean they ran a stop sign. I am talking about liars, murderers, committed incest, adultery, drunkenness, suicide, prostitution, rape, cursing and I could go on and on. I think you get the picture. Most of these men and women, were people who believed in the coming Messiah or were witnesses of Jesus himself. And I am here to tell you that God forgives sin. That was his mission to pay the penalty that Almighty God said the death. His son Jesus did what he came to do on the cross of calvary. Romans 3:23 (KJV) tells us "But the wages of sin is death." Those sins I just mentioned are not usually the sins that hinder the local church. Those sins, we really don't see them as sins. Gossip, jealousy, backbiting, malice, bitterness, strife, these are the little foxes that spoil the vine. I don't care how long you have been out of church God forgives sin. I don't care how old you are God forgives sin. I am not interested in what race, nationality, sex, or country of origin you are God forgives sin. There is a beautiful song that many groups have sung which says, "I'm Just a Sinner Saved by Grace" and for this cause he came into the world to save and to forgive sin. Whether you are an unbeliever or one of his own. I will sum it up with 1 Timothy 1:15 (KJV) *"This is a faithful saying and worthy of all acceptance that Christ Jesus came into the world to save sinners of whom I am chief."*

2. All Have the Same Flesh

Just because you are a new creation in Christ Jesus does not mean that the old man with all its desires goes away. If you have been saved for any length of time you will realize that your flesh still desires to sin. You do not have to teach a child to do wrong, you have to train them to do right. I will not need to write very much here, for you to understand, that each person is capable of doing anything when they allow the flesh to rule over their being. And don't as I have already said, compare your walk with someone else's. I was only seventeen years old when I started preaching. There was at the time, a preacher I'll call him Slim. I listened to Slim preach and I knew that if I watched him enough and listened to his tapes enough, I could be another Slim. People, Slim could out preach any person I had ever heard. And I wanted to be just like Slim. I bought the same suits, and I wore the same shoes. I combed my hair like Slim and I could listen to him preach all day, every day. I thought there was no one in the world like Slim . He was my hero as far as preachers were concerned. One day I heard that Slim had been caught in adultery and his family broke up. Slim had to leave the ministry all together. I was completely devastated about Slim. I still love Slim. If he called and needed money, I would borrow it, if I did not have it to give to him. Because Slim is still my friend. Thankfully, God showed me that he called me to preach like me, not like Slim. As the years rolled by, I knew how Slim fell into adultery. I have preached many revivals in my ministry and one of the traps that Satan tries to get preachers into, is the sin of adultery. Women for some reason are drawn to preachers. I have tried to have my wife Donna explain it to me, but I still do not completely understand. I am as ugly as ugly can be. In the Websters dictionary under the word ugly you see Doug Rowland. But the rest of my forty-five years in the ministry, I preach like Doug and not like Slim. We both have the same desires and weaknesses, that is just not one of mine. Turn in your Bible and read Romans 7:15-25. When you are finished reading, you will see what I mean by we all have the same flesh. Paul was very simply saying the things I should be doing I don't do. And the things I should not be doing I find myself doing. He then hit the nail on the head.

3. All Have the Same Freedom

You may at times be tempted to say no one has ever been through what I have . I will not use the word liar because I want you to buy my next book too . But you are being deceived into thinking in self – pity. However dear reader thousands of people have been where you are in that way of thinking. Allow me to try and explain what I mean about freedom and forgiveness. There is a law called the law of sowing and reaping. Galatians 6:7 (ESV) *"do not be deceived God is not mocked for whatever a man sows that will he also reap for the one who sows that will he also reap for the one who sows to his own flesh will from the flesh reap corruption but the one who sows to the Spirit will from the spirit reap eternal life."* Let us look at this in a way you may understand . You are reaping now what you sowed days, weeks, months, or years ago. And precious reader please understand that this is a law that cannot be broken. Illustration: if I took a razor and cut off my hand in a drunken state, would God forgive me for being drunk? Yes, most definitely, he will forgive me. Will he forgive me from cutting off my hand? Yes. Again, God will forgive me for cutting off my hand. Again, I tell you yes, he will forgive me. Will his forgiveness grow my hand back? I am very sorry but no he will not. Sin has consequences and though he loves you and me, the law of sowing and reaping will never be broken. Does God cast us out from being his child when we as Christians sin, even live in sin? No, once you have been born-again, that settles it. You cannot be born-again time after time, any more than you can enter your mother's womb a second time and be born physically again. When we blow it, that is the place the enemy has his chance to confuse you as a Christian. He will bring guilt rather than conviction. Then if that does not work, he starts planting thoughts in your mind like, you would not have done that if you were really saved; God will not forgive you for that again; what are people going to say when they find it out? We don't have time to go over many tricks of his trade. But he will capitalize on anything he can. You are free to live anyway you want to. But like my dear friend, the late Bobby Grubbs said, "If you live for God he will take you home and crown you, if you don't live for him he will crown you and take you home." So, you are free to live anyway you wish but there is a consequence for every decision.

4. All Have the Same Friends

I have great news for you, you are not the only one to mess up, blow it, or fall into sin. I believe if you could get all this chapter in its proper context you would shout GLORY! Many of the people that you may have thought were beyond sin are people who did the worse things . There is not enough in this book to dwell on much of these and I can't list them all, but let's look at a few, who like us has blown it.

Lot Vexed his Righteous Soul

Lot was the nephew of Abraham and they had a falling out. Abraham gave Lot the choice of the land he wanted . Lot saw the well-watered plains of Sodom, but not the sin underneath .The Grass is never greener over the cesspool. Lot chose Sodom, but not the sinfulness and homosexuality underneath. He left the land by God's command and his wife looked back in direct disobedience to her husband and she turned into a pillar of salt according to Genesis chapter 19.

Abraham Lies About his Wife

In Genesis chapter 12 there was a great famine that came in the land. Abraham was forced to go down to Egypt land in order to find food. Sarai was a very beautiful women to look upon . Abraham was scared that if they knew she was his wife, they would kill him to have Sarai become one of their wives. Abraham told them to say that Sarai was not his wife. But to say that she was his sister. That way they would not kill him nor would they kill Sarai. Abraham was the man that God made a covenant with and he was called the friend of God. This was the man that prepared to sacrifice Isaac upon the mountain, in an act of obedience to God, but God spared him. This great, great, man of faith, wisdom and obedience told not just a white lie, because there is no such thing. He lied straight out. Yes, he knew it and no matter who you are, in the Bible a sin is a sin. If you turn over to Genesis 26:6-8 latter on Isaac does the same thing.

Moses Killed a Person and Smote the Rock

Moses in Exodus 2:11-15 saw an Egyptian being evil to an Israelite and smote him, then buried him in the sand. Understand, murder is murder, and he would have been convicted. In Exodus 20: 11 God told Moses to speak to the rock. But rather than speaking, in anger, he smote the rock. This act of disobedience kept him from going into the promise land. Remember that God told him to merely *speak* to the rock to have water. This was direct disobedience of God. What if God did the same today when we sin? At one direct disobedience, God would kill at once. Every believer ought to be thankful for God's grace and mercy. This is strange, but we do not know the relationship between God and Moses.

David Lying, Committing Adultery and Murder

In 2 Samuel chapters 11 and 12, we find the recording of David. King David in the evening looked, lingered, and lusted over Bathsheba bathing. He sent for her and committed adultery and a son was conceived. He then lied to cover it up. Because of his failed plan, he sent orders that Uriah (her husband) was to be put in the forefront of the hottest battle. Then his soldiers were to retire from him that him, causing him to be smitten and die. Samuel the prophet pointed out the plan. Samuel then shared what God revealed to him with David. This was the time appointed to reveal David's sin. David paid for his sin, because as we have learned the law of sowing and reaping cannot be broken. You can read about the consequences of David's sin in 2 Samuel chapters 12 and 13.

Many More who were Righteous and Sinned

Peter denied the Lord Jesus three times, Thomas doubted him, Rahab was a harlot, Paul broke fellowship with Mark, Jonah refused to go to Nineveh, and Samson told a secret that should have been kept to himself. You see all these people and more, that went in direct opposition to what God said, in short, they blew it. And guess what, they are listed in Hebrews chapter 11 in God's faith hall of fame . You may blow it from time to time. The key is to confess it, repent of it, and put your shoe back on and finish the race that is set before us. As it is written in Hebrews 12 :1 (ESV) *"therefore since we are surrounded with so great a cloud of witness let us also lay aside every weight and the sin which clings so closely and let us run with endurance the race that is set before us."* One trick the enemy uses is to make you feel like there are too many things in the word to do or not do. But just allow the Holy Spirit to live the Christian life through you. Because if you try in your own flesh it will be what's called, performance-based Christianity. It says God will love me more if I do this or that, and don't do this or that. No matter how far you may stray, Jesus loves you with an eternal love, based simply on the fact that you are his creation.

10

SOMEBODY HAS TO MILK THE COWS

ECCLESIASTES 9:10

In Psalms 84:10 (KJV) states *"For a day in thy courts is better than a thousand. I had rather be a doorkeeper in the house of my God, than to dwell in the tens of wickedness."* David was simply saying I would rather be doing something small and menial in the house of God, than to be a big wig in the tents. Pride and ego and attention are some things many people desire even if they do not mean to. It's normal to want recognition for the things we do. I heard of one man who loved attention that if he went to a funeral, he would get jealous of the corpse. Now that goes beyond the normal yearning for wanting attention. God has a place for everyone, and he wants everyone in their place. And there is a problem when you are out of your place. God has chosen for you a place in his kingdom. And in the church, there are a lot of things that needs to be done. We need to find our place in the church and do it, whether it be something big or something that people do not even notice when it has been done. Now the church is compared to three things: a body, a building and a bride.

The Church as a Body

The body, or the little earth suits that God has given to us, has members that some are seen, and some parts are unseen. Now what if my big toe got mad at my index finger, because my toe did not get seen like my finger did? God, according to the Bible says, in Psalms 139 (KJV) *"We are fearfully and wonderfully made."* God made these bodies, so that each part inside and outside, seen or unseen, has a place and a job to perform. Just like in the local church. Everyone, and I mean everyone, has a place to fit in the church. You say all I do is attend and go home. I will give an answer to that as we go further into this chapter.

The Church as a Building

The Bible says in 1 Peter 2:6 (KJV) *"... Jesus is the chief cornerstone..."* Since Jesus is the chief corner stone, then we are the bricks, that are made, to build the church. Every single person who gets saved is a part of the universal church. Most every brick is different. Underneath the bricks are cinder blocks that from the outside may not be seen. But they are vital to keep the building in its place. Since that is true, we that are saved are the ones that add to the church such as should be saved.

The Church as a Bride

Jesus Christ looks at the church, as his church, his bride. And his desire for his bride, is to be without spot or wrinkle, as he presents the bride to God. But in a wedding, having the dress is not all there is to a wedding. There are a lot of behind the scenes things that the people don't even know about. And without people taking care of small things, the wedding will be a flop. The same is true for the church. Without people doing the little things the church will crumble .

With that in mind, I want to tell you a story in my that actually happened in my life. I was only thirteen years old, when my parents wanted to go to Florida. We had been there the year before and I had had enough of Florida. So, my uncle and aunt had a farm, with a big pond loaded with bass and trout. They also had a horse that I had been on and rode many times. I ask my parents to let stay with them so I could fish, ride the horse and play in the barn. Well that's not what happened! I pegged five acres of tobacco. If you don't know what that is, here's what you do. My uncle woke me up at five o'clock. Not in the evening but in the morning. We got on the tractor and went to the brown dirt and I was handed a peg eight inches long and two inches around. I asked my uncle what it was for. He said in his slow southern draw, well you take the piece of wood and thrust it in the ground. I will come in behind you and drop the tobacco plants in. Five acres, five, out in the hot sun, down on my knees. Pegging five acres of these plants over a period of four days. On Monday when it started, I thought I will get to go fishing later. We went to supper and I thought now I will get to go fishing. No way, we had a cattle ramp we had to build. All week it was pegging, building a new cattle ramp, or cleaning out the barn I got to fish zero times. I got to ride Cookie the horse zero times. But all of that paled in comparison to Wednesday morning at five o'clock. That was the day that will go down in infamy. That morning my uncle had an early errand to run and I had the great honor of milking the cows. I knew nothing about milking a cow. What, do you do pump the tail up and down till milk comes out? Well Duh! I sat on my little seat and tried to milk the cows. It took me one and a half hours to milk that 1 cow and I still had four more to go. My uncle got back from his errand and saw that there was more milk on the ground than in the buckets. I still recall him belly laughing at me. But somebody had to milk the cows. At the end of the week he gave me two fifty cent pieces. One dollar for all that pegging on my knees five acres of land. One dollar for helping build a cattle ramp and cleaning out an old barn.

What did I learn from that? Well first off, I love Florida a lot more than I did before. I learned that farming is hard work. And I learned that some things are glorious, and somethings can wait. But I learned that somebody has to milk the cows no matter what else gets done. Now let's see how this makes sense in the spiritual world.

Somebody has to be the Director

A nation cannot make it with two presidents, a home cannot be a home with two people who make decisions, and a church will never prosper with two pastors running the show. I think about the churches I pastored before going into evangelism. I pastored one where I thought the deacon board ran the church more than the me. I thought I better not bring up anything, or as young as I am, I will get fired. I soon found out the church ran the church. These men of God wanted to do anything that they believed would honor God. In that church was one of my best friends still today, Tracy Duval, my youth director. I cannot think of one thing the church did not let us do. We were able to do about anything we wanted to do. Dear reader, your pastor has a load to carry. You may even disagree with something he does and think I will find me a different church. If you are looking for the perfect pastor, you better buy you a camper because you are going to be moving a lot. The pastor should be well taken care of money wise. And remember he is just a human, like you, but with a different calling in life. In a church I pastored, a young preacher attended there, whom I really loved and watched him grow very much. But as much as I liked this guy, he tried to literally gain a following. One Sunday he asked if he could say a word before I was to preach. But it was a lot more than a word. This guy kept on and on until noon that day. We needed to have a talk. It was one of the hardest things I ever had to do. If I was wrong, then this young man would more than likely leave the church with his followers and that would be bad for me. If I was right it could have split the church into pieces. So, after the service I asked him to meet me in my office and I confronted him. I was right, he said I was not spiritual enough to be the pastor and he wanted me out. To make a long story short, I had to reveal this to the church body. I asked him to repent. I then took one of my deacons with me to his house on two different times. The night of the business meeting he would not repent and after a vote of the church body he was asked to leave until he could see his wrong- doing. It was 100% unanimous for him to go . He got up and said any of you that are with him he would be starting a new church . He thought there would be 30-40 people walk out with him. When no one left, I said to the young man you will be welcomed back upon your repentance. Two weeks later this vital young man died with cancer he did not even know he had. What I am saying is the pastor should be the leader, but not a dictator. But none the less, the leader is not to be led by deacons or anyone else. In 3 JOHN verse 9-11 We read about a man named Diotrephes who basically wanted to run the church and if anyone went against him, he wanted them voted out. Somebody has got to be THE leader. Not *a* leader, but *the* leader. A person who allows the people to run him, is not a pastor, he is just a preacher. Yes, the pastor gets attention: yes, he wears a suit (unless you go to a church where they preach in jeans, t-shirt and flip flops). I believe the pastor needs to look the part. And those who dress that way, I can have complete fellowship with. But I think the pastor should look, live and labor as God's man. And if you have fried preacher more than fried chicken, you are out of line and need to confess that as sin. If you have a problem with the preacher go to him and spell it out. But it is a lot easier for you to move your letter, than for a preacher to move his family. His main job is not visiting people, it is preaching the word .

Somebody must do the Dirty Work

It is no fun getting up at five in the morning, it be raining, cold, even snowing, to milk a bunch of living hamburgers. But it must be done each and every day. There are some jobs in the church that are done without anyone even knowing it was done. Somebody has to keep the nursery, some are Sunday School teachers, piano and organ players, choir and singing directors, ushers, and deacons. Someone has got to do these things. Somebody has to be treasurer. Now I want to say something here. The treasurer is nothing more than someone other than the pastor, to disperse the money. They have no business thinking that they should have any more say over the money than anyone else. I had a treasurer who thought that it was her money and that she was the one who owned it. You pastors that have that kind of a person in that position, you need to put someone else in. A good way to remedy this is by having a rotating treasurer's position. Now that brings me to really milking the cows. In our church because it is so huge, the administrative positions are a full-time job. But in most churches, someone must mow and weed eat, make sure the songbooks and pew bibles are placed in places where people are seated in the congregation. Someone has to paint, work on the roof, replace broken glass. Still others might need to make sure the baptistry is full when it's time to baptize people. Others may work on the church bulletin, clean the toilets, sweep the carpet and mop the floors. If you have a fellowship hall, make sure it's clean and trash is taken out. There are so many jobs that needs to be filled in the church, so it is run right, that there is no reason why there should ever be something left undone. Granted it may not be a job where you get a pat in the back. But as I said someone has to milk the cows. And by the way the one who scrubs the toilet will be rewarded for faithfulness just as much the preacher in his calling . See it is not what we do, it all hinges on our faithfulness to what we do. Judges 7:21 (KJV) says *"And they stood every man in his place."* I am a believer in that every person has a place. You say preacher Doug I am old and can't do anything. Oh, yes you can! Somebody has to pray and be a prayer warrior! As a matter of fact, those who can't do manual labor, or are not cut out to be an usher, or whatever, here's a suggestion. Start a Bible study in your home, cook a meal for someone who needs it because of a death in the family, or sickness and on and on. Be creating your own prison ministry. Somebody has to do the milking in every church!

Somebody has to be Dedicated

In being a part of a church, anything you do, you have to have a certain amount of dedication. Even if no one sees what you are doing, be dedicated to that cause. A pig and a chicken decided to do something nice for the farmer who had been so good to them down through the years. They thought and thought . Finally, the chicken said let's cook a meal for him and give him breakfast in bed. The pig said that's a good idea what shall we fix him. The chicken said let's fix ham and eggs . The pig said oh no! With you it is just a donation, with me it is complete dedication! In Ecclesiastes 9:10 (KJV) we read *"Whatsoever thy hand findeth to do, do it with thy might; for there is no work, nor device, nor knowledge, nor wisdom in the grave whither thou goest."*

Somebody has to be Designated

I am simply saying you need to be matched up with ever what cow you decide to milk. Let the pastor know what is in your heart to do so there be no surprises. But the Bible says whatever you do, do it with all your heart and strength and might. There are some people that are out front, and there are some that you never see. However, in a big church or small church, somebody has to milk the cows. What about you? What cow will you milk?

11

OK NOW WHAT AM I GOING TO DO

PROVERBS 3:5 AND 6

I suppose this is one of the best-known scriptures found in the Bible. I can remember in Sunday School some of the teachers making us memorize these two verses in Proverbs. These two verses could be used when making decisions. As a matter of fact, the smartest man that ever lived wrote this many years ago. Other than my own personal devotions, I read a chapter in Proverbs every day. Doing this will eventually begin to find its way down deep and find that the wisdom given has value that money cannot buy. It is said that we make from 2,000 to 3,500 decisions a day. I laughed at that figure amount when I first read this fact. However, when you think about it, we make decisions that we don't even realize we are making. When to shower, how long to let the grass grow, how much do I give at church, what's for supper, what will I wear today, and on and on. I think as far as our Christian walk goes this is the most important chapter in this book. Bad decisions lead to what I call, the spiritual yo-yo effect. One day you are up and happy, the next day you are down and pouting. We make decisions in different ways. Some people will flip a coin, others will draw straws. And have you ever prayed Lord, if this is OK to do let it rain tomorrow? There are so many verses in the Bible about making the right decisions. Being a pastor the for the first half of my forty-five years in the ministry was very hard, especially while in my twenties. Because most of the deacons, ushers, trustees and even my youth director, were older than me. The enemy told me if I made a decision that they did not agree with, they would think I was too young to make such decisions. God began to deal with my heart, that he was the one who led me into the ministry. And if they went against something I felt was spiritually for the good for the church, he would deal with them. He used Proverbs 3:5 and 6 to enlighten me to this fact. But what questions should we ask before making big decisions . I am not talking about whether to have a Big Mac or quarter pounder . I'm talking about life's choices that effects more than just you a bigger way . What are some of these questions ?

Will This Decision Glorify God

1Corinthians 10:31(KJV) *"Whether therefore Ye eat, or drink, or whatsoever ye do, do all to the glory of God."* I put this one first because it should be the first question, we ask ourselves, when making big life decisions. Can God get glory if I buy this do that, take this job, or whatever it is. Can God get glory out of this or that decision. Dear reader I am not talking about decisions that do not radically change your life. God does not care about the kind of water hose or pantyhose you get. But we are talking about choices that would involve you and or others. Does my choice glorify Jesus or not?

Could I ask God to Bless my Decision

Proverbs 14:14 (ESV) *"The backslider in heart will be filled with the fruit of his ways, and a good man will be filled with the fruit of his ways."* This is simply saying the man who walks in the flesh cannot be blessed by walking in the flesh and receive good fruit. But the good man can ask God to bless the fruit of his decisions and be blessed with good fruit.

Maybe you are trying to buy a house, though it is out of your price range. To buy it you must take a second job taking away time to get involved at church. Family time goes down the drain. You either have to work on Sunday or you are too tired to go to church. Yes, you may have a great house, but the things that make up a home are gone. Can you ask God to bless your decision? I would think that God could not bless a choice like this.

Does What I do Cause Harm to the Testimony of Myself and my Church

I believe that any decision I make, I must remember that people on the outside look at Christians with a microscope and the church as well. Have you ever heard this? Oh, all they are down there at that church is a bunch of hypocrites. More than likely it is just an excuse for not going anywhere to Gods house. But sadly, there are times when they are right. Psalms 37:23 (KJV) says *"The steps of a good man are ordered of the Lord."* We need to look deep down and see if where I work, get my groceries, everyone in your circle of daily or monthly acquaintances, know you are a Christian. I'm afraid that people take church membership to lightly. People will not go to a church where there is fussing and fighting. If you are saved by God's grace and a member of a local church, you have a responsibility to live a Godly life every day. Showing the world that your church is a special place where God is worshiped, and the Bible is preached.

How will this Decision Affect my Family

I will not be saying much about this point. To use an illustration, that is a true story, will get the point across. After church one Sunday, a man came up to me and said he would like to talk to me before church on that Wednesday night. I said that would be fine. Wednesday night came and he sat down. Now up to this point, both the man and his wife taught in Sunday School. His children were active in the youth group. He said pastor, we will be moving in a few weeks. I asked him where they were going. He told me he was moving to another state. He said he was offered more money and a few extra benefits if he would take the job promotion . I asked him how much he had prayed about it. And he sort of smiled and said well, with more money I can take better care of my family. He would find a church there and get involved there. I told him of how pulling the kids out of the school they loved would be hard for them. He said they will make new friends there. This man's family, even the wife did not feel like it would be a good move and that they were living good where they lived. Truth be told he had more possessions than anyone else in the church. But with practically no prayer and the family not wanting to move, they moved anyway. I really prayed hard before I told him I thought he was making a mistake to move, but to no avail. Within one year they were no longer in church. Having more money, he went into debt even more, to where the wife had to go back to work. The eldest boy in the family got into wearing black Gothic stuff and the teenage daughter got pregnant. This man payed a huge for price what for he thought was the right thing to do. Precious reader the greatest thing I can think of is a good and happy family. Whatever you are having to make a decision about, make sure you see how it might affect your family life. Romans14:7(KJV) *"For none of us liveth to himself and no man dieth to himself."* The actions we take almost always carry with it, consequences that will affect ourselves and our families.

Is There a Bible Answer to Your Decisions

If you look hard enough, you will find the answer to life's major decisions in the pages of God's Holy word the Bible. Psalms 119:10 (ESV*) says "With my whole heart I seek you; let me not wander from your commandments."* Verse 66 (ESV) says *Teach me good judgement and knowledge for I believe your commandments."* In the same chapter, verse 105 "Your word is a lamp unto my feet and a light to my path." The Bible is so rich with counsel that you can find the answer to anything clearly if you just study long enough. Allow it to speak to you in your special place. Because of a failed back surgery, I can no longer sleep in a regular bed. My bedroom is big enough for a recliner to fit next to our bed. My wife Donna can be asleep in 30 seconds Thus my prayer closet is a nice big recliner. The car, the den, the literal closet can be that special place where you meet with God. He is the great I am and will answer every prayer we pray. We may not like the answer, but God does answer every prayer we pray, as long as it meets God's will for your life. If you cannot find the answer between the pages of the Bible, it may be best for you not to change anything. My papaw Clay Rowland always said if you are in doubt, then don't!

Do I Have Peace in my Heart

There is nothing on earth spiritually and emotionally, like having peace and to know that 100 percent of that peace is from God. Actually, there are three kinds of peace mentioned in the Bible.

Peace with God. Romans *5:1 (KJV) says "Therefore being justified by faith we have peace with God through our Lord Jesus Christ."* This kind of faith is the peace we have when we get born again. Faith alone, not faith plus works, church membership or anything else. Faith alone in the blood atoning death of Jesus Christ on the cross, being buried in a tomb, and He rose again the third day. When that happens, there is peace **with** God. Next is for the Christian that may be going through a storm, temptation, or some trial. We call this, not peace with God, but the peace **of** God. Isaiah 26:3 (KJV) says *" Thou wilt keep him in perfect peace whose mind is stayed on thee."*

Readers, you really need to turn to Philippians 4:5-7(KJV). the little phrase, "…and the peace of God." There are going to be times when storms of life are going to press us down to the point of total despair. I know what I am about to say is easier said than done. But for me at least it has never let me down. Do what the word instructs to do in the verses I have given you. And I think 90 percent of what we are worried about does not come to pass. And the other 10 percent is not as bad as we thought it would be. Lastly in the Bible, is not peace with God, or peace of God, but it is peace on earth good will to man. Luke 2:14 (KJV) says *"Glory to God in the highest and on earth peace good will toward men."* One day this heaven and earth shall pass away, and a new heaven and earth will be created. And there will be peace **on** earth. But any decisions we make, we need to ask God to give us peace about what we are about to choose. Would the decisions alter our walk with God?

Is There a Hidden Selfish Motive

When we are faced with making big decisions, look way, way, down deep in your heart and see if maybe there is a selfish motive. My dad was a car man and he loved cars. I was ten years old when we moved from Pennsylvania. back to Virginia Daddy said we needed a new car . Now remember he was only thirty years old He left one morning to trade cars. In about an hour he came back with a brand, new Ford mustang, blue with white racing stripes. You that are car guys, will like this; it had mag wheels and raised white letter tires. It was a 390 engine and four-barrel carburetor, with a four-speed manual transmission WEEE Dogggggies that was super hot! The inside was black leather bucket seats. My mom came out to see the car. Now remember, there were three young boys born at the time. Mom told dad how pretty it was and how fast it would go. They asked us three boys to try and get in the back seat. We could barely sit in it. Mom said, now Doug, you go and find a family car and grow up. When he pulled out on the road in the Mustang, that car turned the tires in all four gears. About three hours later he came home with a new four door Pontiac. Dad made a bad selfish move. Yes, we needed a car, but not one that could win the Daytona 500. When making any decision, make sure your motives are in line both with the Bible and the Holy Spirit.

What Will I have to Give Up

When making life altering decisions ask yourself what you would have to give up in order to do what you are deciding to do. Now I know there are many good churches everywhere. But if you are in a church where you are getting fed well, by a conservative Bible preacher, think hard about a location move. I know it is hard to do at times, but your spirit man is far more important than the little earth suit man we live in. What indeed would you have to let go of in your decision? Notice James 4:2 b and 3 (KJV) *"Yet ye have not because ye ask not, ye ask and receive not because ye ask amiss that ye may consume it upon your lust."* The American dream can be a nightmare when we make decisions that are not backed up through the leading of the Holy Spirit and the scriptures.

What are the Priorities in my Life

All of us have made very bad decisions in life. Oh, how I wish I could go back and do more with what God has given me. And to undo, some very dumb as a river rock decision on the other hand. But the good news is that we serve a forgiving, long suffering, patient Savior. One who is a Savior of a second, third, and fourth chances. Ask yourself what are the priorities in my life? Is it a big house, luxury automobile, money, or power? And there is not **one** thing wrong with any of those things. But seek ye **first** God's kingdom and the rest will come in due time. Beloved, ever so often I like to take a little checkup and ask myself what am I trying to accomplish with my life? One day I am going to die as you are also. And I want to hear the words, *well done thy good and faithful servant. Enter into the joys of the Lord.*

12

NAOMI THE MATCHMAKER

RUTH CHAPTERS 1-4

This is a story of Naomi, whose life was filled with sorrow and heart ache. It gives us a part of the blood line of Jesus Christ. It also shows us five different ways of drawing closer to Jesus. I personally am of the right opinion, that if a person is truly saved by the blood of Jesus, that person should have the desire to grow closer to God each day. I know that you and I are going to have days when we don't even feel saved So that's why I say, do not measure your growth with someone else's spiritual measuring stick. Brethren use Jesus as your measuring stick. I think it bears repeating that you and I only see most Christians at church we don't know what another person may being be going through during the week. Some of the people we think are on top of the world spiritually, are the ones that may be carrying the biggest burdens or going through the hardest storms.

As we get into this story in the Old Testament. we will see how it relates for us in the new testament. Remember God wants to see real growth in our life. Whether it be one-eighth or five miles in our spiritual growth. Before we get into the main story, we need to lay down a foundation on Naomi's match making and how to draw closer in our daily walk with Jesus. Let us notice three things.

Notice a Famine

Bethlehem was in bad shape because there was no food. Word reaches the people that there was food in Moab. This family gathers up their things and heads to Moab. When we start to get will hungry, we will do whatever we can to get some food. We are in a famine for hearing the gospel preached. The gospel in the Bible is the death, burial and resurrection of Jesus. However, we would not have much of it (spiritual food that is), or be reached by it, from watching Christian TV. We would hear how to give them our money and be healed from anything and if we gave them all of our money, we would have all the money we needed. So, we are having a famine of preachers, who just preach the gospel.

Notice a Family

Naomi had a husband named Elimelech, and two sons named Mahlon and Chilion. And while they were in Moab, the sons took Gentile brides named Orpah and Ruth. Over the process of ten years Elimelech, Mahlon, and Chilion died and left all three women as widows. Naomi wanted to go back to Bethlehem. Naomi told the girls to go back to their homes, to the point of begging for them to go home and start their lives over. Finally, Orpah went her own way. But Ruth he famous words in in Ruth 1:16 (KJV) *"And Ruth said intreat me not to leave thee or to return from following after thee: For whither thou goest I will go and whither thou lodgest I will lodge: Thy people shall be my people and thy God my God."* Ruth loved Naomi with a deep love and wanted to be with her anywhere she went. Though she was a Gentile and Naomi a Jew. Bill Gaither wrote a song with words of: "I'm So Glad I'm a part of the family of God." I am also glad that I have been redeemed by the blood of Jesus and am a part of one great big group of people, who one day will be reunited with the ones who have gone on before us.

Notice a Fortune

It just happened Naomi's dead husband had a relative named Boaz in the city. Seeing that Naomi and Ruth were very poor, he gave them a job threshing the wheat and barley. Of course, as we get into this story, we will see the hand of God in all the events in this story. But seeing Ruth was still a young woman, still capable of bearing children, Naomi plays the role of matchmaker in getting them together. This union of Ruth and Boaz leads to marriage. As a result, we have Obed, their son, who was directly in the blood line of David, thru which is the direct line of none other than Jesus Christ himself. Now as I said, Naomi plays the matchmaker between Ruth and Boaz in Ruth Chapter 3, verses 3, 4 and 5 And these same scriptures will be five things that will draw us closer to God himself. The advice that was given by Naomi sounds for the most part, how a young lady would be getting ready for a date today. Her advice was simple.

1. Be Freshly Cleaned. Verse 3 "Wash Thyself"

Naomi's first suggestion was for her to take a good bath. I have had a few dates in my life until I met my wife at age 19. Three of which were set up by a preacher friend of mine. But I never had one date that I felt that the girl never took a bath. The point is, you will never get close to God when you have a bunch of unconfessed sin in your life. Before I can begin to ask God for anything, dear reader I have to agree with God about sin. If someone wrote down a list for an order when you pray, I believe that number one on the list would be to confess your sins God cannot look upon, or over, any sin that maybe dwelling in our lives. The scriptures declare *"If I regard iniquity in my heart the lord will not hear me."* The Bible does not lie concerning sin in our lives. Open sin in the life of the person who has truly been born-again cannot be tolerated by a righteous and holy God. Again, the Psalms of David echo *"Save me from presumptuous sin."* That is sin that we fall into at every temptation that comes. Those sins we wish were not sins. I ask you what is that sin, though you confess it, you have trouble repenting from it? I have mentioned this several times in this book. And may I say that if not repented of, is the one absolutely, the only thing, that keeps you from that sweet fellowship with our creator. The attitude of "O well we are not perfect" is the wrong attitude to have. The problem is, you are right, we are not perfect, but no one tries to be either. I may be the only person in the world to believe in this, but we need to have a heart that is sensitive not just to the Holy Spirit. But we need to be sensitive to sin when it has been committed. Listen carefully, not all sin is the sin of drinking to the point of slobbering all over yourself, visiting a prostitute, main lining heroine, cursing like a sailor, or deceiving your spouse. What about jealousy, gossip, backbiting, bitterness, anger, malice and temper . Before I had my ankle injury, which required three surgeries I could walk and get around pretty good. The injury put me in a wheelchair for most of the time. Before the injury, I loved yard work. I loved mowing, weed eating, and cleaning my cars. I looked forward to doing it every week. In one of the houses we lived in, before my injury, I was mowing the yard. There were two places in our yard that would not grow grass. No matter what we did, it would not grow any type of grass or even weeds for that matter. So, when I would mow, I would always get a good dirt bath. One day it was exceptionally hot. I sweated like a turkey on thanksgiving eve. I got my dirt bath mixed with sweat. I also, on that day, had two vehicles to clean. We were trying to sell one of the vehicles. It was about six o'clock in the evening before I was finished. Donna, my wife, was all cleaned up waiting for me to get a bath, then we were going out to eat. I came in the house sweaty, dirty and smelling like a boiled egg buried in a jar of cabbage. I ran up to her and said give me a kiss sweetie and a big hug. No indeed! You get a bath first she told me. I ran her from room to room trying to get her to kiss and hug . Finally, I got a bath, and we went out to eat. But first I got my hug and kiss. The Bible says *"Now you are clean through the word."* The Bible is like a mirror, it will show you where you have the dirt, sweat, and sin. To be close to God we must be clean. When is the last time you allowed the word to speak to you and you agreed with God, about some unconfessed sin in your walk with Him?

2. Be Fragrantly Consecrated, Anoint Thee

In Biblical times you must remember that people did not get up and head for the shower. They did not have garden tubes or tubes with jets in them. The one thing they did keep clean was their hands and their feet. They may get a bath every week or every two weeks. That was the reason Naomi told her once you get a bath, put on something that will make you smell really good. I did not tell you what else I had done on the day I chased Donna around the house. I shaved put on both after shave and cologne. When I came out of that bathroom into the bedroom, I got my hug and kiss from my beautiful wife. Naomi told Ruth, you go and anoint yourself. My wife puts on perfume in a very unusual way. Rather than take a little dab behind each ear, or maybe putting some on each wrist, she sprays it out into mid- air and walks thru the mist of it. Years ago, deodorant was in a spray can. I thought, is that the way she used to put on deodorant spray? Spray it into the air and move her arms up and down. Anyway, Naomi wanted Ruth to have an aroma around her. I said already in this book, that the Holy Spirit is to us, what Jesus was to his disciples. God wants his people to have a walk with his people in the person of the Holy Spirit. For a very short period of six years, I pastored a full-time gospel singing group called the Primitive Quartet. Their name comes from the fact that they used guitars, mandolins, an upright bass and banjo's. They were as I am, a regular ole run of the mill Baptist, not being in a Primitive Baptist denomination. The leader of the group was Reagan Riddle. Reagan said one day, "You know you can tell if a person is walking in the spirit. That has never left me since that day and helped me make it through one of the darkest places of my entire life. And what a perfect statement it was to say that you can tell when a person is walking in the spirit. And that is the one thing in the Christians life that cannot be manufactured. A person can go to church, and say the right words, but there is a certain aura around a person who is saved by grace and seeking the face of God. This kind of aura has with it, a humble spirit that yields with it, the fruits of the spirit. Are you the type person, that when in normal everyday life, you have passed someone, and you do not have ask that important question of are you a Christian or not? It is answered. To get closer to God each one of us need to be walking in the spirit.

3. Be Fitly Clothed, Put thy Raiment upon Thee

Naomi's advice to Ruth was to go and get the fitly clothed. In other words, Ruth you go and put on your best dress. Don't you go down there in jeans and an old sweatshirt? The Bible was really adamant about what we should put on. First, we go to Ephesians 6:10-18. From *"finally my brethren,"* to the words *"Praying always,"* let these scriptures be our clothing. But more important, than putting on the whole armor of God, is found in Romans 13: 14 (KJV) *"But put ye on the Lord Jesus Christ and make not provision for the flesh to fulfill the lust thereof.* The word does not lie, no matter what skeptics may say. Because if you put on Christ you have put on all that he is. As the song says, "Victory in Jesus in Jesus my Savior forever." Look also in Ephesians 4:22-24 (KJV) Paul writes almost word for word what he says to the Romans. He says to put off the old man (Ruth's jeans and sweatshirt) and put on the new man (nice pretty dress). We as Christians today need to keep ourselves dressed at all times, putting on Jesus first before you even get out of bed. Walking in the flesh will sooner or later (more sooner) will keep you from the word. You will begin to quit praying as you at one time you did. When you quit reading the Word and studying, you will start missing church . Then you will starve the spiritual man and eventually you will quit church altogether. Our enemy knows if you starve the spiritual man you will be another one, on the devil's list, that he can put a check mark on, as being spiritually A.W.O.L! And how shall we escape if we neglect so great salvation. In 1 Peter 1:8 guarantees that if we do the math in verses 4 and 5, that we will always be fruitful and never be barren. Verse 9 tells us that if we do not add to our faith, we could stray so far you would forget you were a child of the King. 1 Timothy 4:1and 2 (ESV) *"Now the spirit says expressly, that in the latter times some shall depart from the faith, giving heed to seducing spirits and doctrines of devils; speaking lies in hypocrisy having their conscience seared with a hot iron."* Paul says in the last days before, the rapture of the church, many would live in such a way that sin no longer will bother their conscience. What a sad statement for Paul to say about people. We are seeing this fulfilled right before our eyes. The day of people who at least respected Christianity, have long since been left lehind. Today Christians are getting the blame for the evil and hate in this world. Christians are laughed at and the world no longer has time for the message of the cross. Billy Graham said the longer time goes by, the harder it will be for those who are redeemed! Before we go on let us agree that by putting on Jesus, we draw us closer to Him.

4. Be Fully Committed

In the book of Ruth chapter 3, and in verse 5, we find that Ruth was willing to do whatever Naomi asked her to do. And as a result of her obedience, she gained a husband and a child in the blood line Jesus Christ . Remember now we are talking about how to get closer to God . Growing up in the South was quite an experience, especially at hog killing day. It was always cold as a mother- in-laws love and there were always neighbors that would drop in and help one another. And the meat of the hog was the meat to take people thru the winter. Ham, bacon, and sausage were awfully good when fried and paired with gravy and hot biscuits. Both my mom and my Mamaw could make the kind of gravy and biscuits that would make your tongue want to slap your eye teeth. One day a preacher came over while people were cutting the hog up for winter. He said to my Papaw, "Sam you know God wants the whole hog not half a hog, he wants the whole hog. That statement has stayed with me for all these years. And I have found it spiritually makes just as much sense. God wants to have all of us to himself, but he wants us to want him. Yes, Jesus wants to be wanted. Many years ago, one of my preacher friends came to my church for a week-long revival. At the same time about six miles from me, my first cousin Ricky McClure, was also having a revival with another evangelist friend of mine. We all decided to eat breakfast together. We got to thinking about playing some golf. Ricky, Don McCann and I decided we would go the next day. We did not ask Bobby if he wanted to go. We thought it was a given that we all were going play golf. Don, Ricky, and I were waiting for Bobby to come out. After about 10 minutes we went to his room and I asked are you ready to go play Bobby? Play what? he asked. I replied, to go play golf. Bobby said Oh! I thought just you three wanted to go. You never said anything about me going. And besides, I am not ready to go play golf. About that time a chewing gum wrapper fell out of Bobby's hands, as he bent down to pick up the wrapper, three golf balls fell out of his jacket pocket. We just started dying of laughter. Bobby wanted to be wanted. Jesus is the same. With Him he wants to be wanted. He is a jealous God, and he wants us fully committed to Him . Psalms 37:5 (KJV) says *"Commit thy way unto the Lord trust also in him and he shall bring it to past."* In Psalms 34:8 (KJV) it says *"O taste and see that the Lord is good. Blessed is the man that trusteth in him."* When King David says commit, he is saying hand it over to him. I Peter 5:7 (KJV) says *"Casting all your care upon him, or he careth or you"* If God cares that much for us, then what are we so worried about, and why don't we commit it all to him?

5. Be Faithfully Compliant 4-7

Ruth tells Naomi when to go down to where Boaz sleeps. But first she should get snazzied up and lay down at his feet. In Biblical days this was a sign of honor and respect. So, Ruth does exactly what Naomi says to do. We desperately need revivals where people are not afraid of doing what Jesus says to do . We are swiftly in a generation where people that claim to be saved no longer are listening to the voice of the Holy Spirit. We give many excuses to not obey God's word; such as: We know the Bible ought to be read and I will get it later, but later never comes; I will pray when I can get alone with God, but you don't ever find that time; I know I need to be faithful to God's house, but I have to visit Mom and Dad every weekend, after all they are getting old, I have to work, or I don't feel do good. Our nation, our schools, and our families, our colleges and our government will be just fine when we are compliant with what God requires of us. Ruth and Boaz got married. As we said before, but it needs to be said one more time, out of this seed of Obed is the blood line of the coming Messiah Jesus Christ. Playing the match maker was perfect for the blood line of Jesus. Naomi's matchmaking skills paid off after all. And that should show us how the Word is precise.

13

FORWARD IS THE BEST GAMBLE

II KINGS 6 AND 7

Many times, we say things that just does not make a lot of sense. And often we think that it came right out of the Bible. For example, "Every dog shall have its day" is not in the scriptures. One of my uncles, before he died, swore the Bible had scripture that said, every tub shall sit on its own bottom. Sounds good, however you will not find it even in the book of Noah.

I have heard it said by some well-meaning people, even preachers "If I had it to do all over again, I would not change a thing." This is well-meaning yet is a very naive and rather shallow statement. As I have said, if I were twenty years old again, there are some of the most ridiculous choices I ever made, and I would gladly make changes. Giving in to the lust of the old flesh and its desire had caused me to make some long-lasting decisions. I would have done a lot different if I had it to do all over again. I love history namely World War II. How the war began and ended, and the different characters that were in that time. Men like of course the devil himself, Adolf Hitler, Dr. Josef Mengele, then we had the heroes with Winston Churchill, Dwight

Eisenhower, and the man with a two-pearl grip handgun, George Patton.

George Patton, though he was a little controversial when he slapped a couple of men, whom he thought needed some encouragement. Then there were remarks he made to various heads of countries. There were two words that he said he never wanted to hear "Retreat" and "We are holding our own." In 2 Kings 7:3-4 we have a story of four lepers who were put in a place of planning a decision. Just for giggles, let's call them Innie, Mennie, Miny and Mo. The decision they had to make was, do we go back to the city where the war is raging, or sit still till we die. Both of these options could, and more likely would, have caused death to all four of them. However, there was a third choice, which was a gamble. That decision was to go forward into enemy territory and take their chances. They agreed that even if it ended in death for them, to move forward was the best gamble.

Benhadad, the King of Syria, was at war with Elisha and the people of Samaria. Samaria was in a small valley of sorts. Rough terrain and mountains were on both sides of the small city. Thus, making it a sort of one way in and one way out scenario. Benhadad was a wise king and figured out the best way conquer Samaria was to encircle the city, cut off weapons, other soldiers, and most of all food from coming in. Soon things began to get very bad in Samaria. Not just for the people there, but also the four lepers Innie, Mennie, Miny, and Moe, who were sitting at the gate of the enemy.

Notice the Design off the Enemy

Our physical bodies need food period. If we do not eat it effects our strength, ability to fight off sickness, our growth and getting proper nutrients to the main parts of our bodies. As a matter of fact, it became so bad in Samaria that strange things began to happen. The spiritual man needs feeding as well.

In order for us to grow in our walk with the Lord Jesus Christ. If our enemies, which are the world, the flesh, and the devil, cut off our food supply, we will get the same symptoms as we do when our bodies are not properly fed . Our emotions come into play so much in our walk with Christ. Many books are written on just dealing with our emotions. When we know we need to spend time in the word and prayer, the enemy will try and cut off that valuable food supply by replacing it with, let's say the obvious, T.V. or using the computer.

When we know we should be listening to Godly music and being faithful to our personal devotions; the enemy will replace it with that hobby we enjoy doing. When it's time for church and being faithful and active in it, the enemy will find us another place to go. We all as Christians need to get fed regularly and recognize when the enemy wants to cut off our spiritual food. 1 Peter 5:8 (ESV)says *"Be sober-minded be watchful your adversary the devil prowls around like a roaring lion seeking someone to devour."*

Notice the Diet of the Hungry

2 Kings 6:25 (ESV) says *"And there was a great famine in Samaria as they besieged it until a donkey's head was sold for eighty shekels of silver and the fourth part of a cup of doves' dung for five shekels of silver."* Now then I don't know about you, but that really does not sound very appetizing. They did not put cheese on it and did not offer any fries to go. It just goes to show, you will eat things when at one time you would have laughed about someone eating it. And if that was not bad enough, look at 2 Kings 6:26-32. Can you imagine for one second killing your child, boiling and eating them? You see when you are not properly fed you will also do things you never thought you would do. However precious believer there's a difference between physical hunger and spiritual hunger. In his book "A Thirst for God" Sherwood Wirt wrote when we're physically hungry, we eat, and we are satisfied. The hunger disappears. But when we're spiritually hungry, we eat and find ourselves hungrier. We discover our appetite for God and his word has increased. That's why a disciplined consistent study of God's word and regular participation

in a Bible-teaching ministry are critical for the growth of our spiritual lives as Christians.

But notice this, when we're physically hungry and miss a meal, we soon feel like we're starving, and we can't wait to eat. In the spiritual realm, it's just the opposite. When we miss our spiritual meals, we begin to lose our appetites. We are in serious danger when we fail to demonstrate a soul that is hungry for God and his wisdom. So, all new readers need desperately, to get and stay on a good spiritual diet.

Notice the Decision of the Lepers

Well here the four lepers are in a famine, and in a war with King Benhadad and the Syrians. But Innie. Mennie, Miny and Moe must come up with an answer and make a decision. Just like every believer must daily make a choice and decide if I am going back to sin and misery, just do nothing but sit still spiritually, or are you going to get up in the morning and say Jesus let's go forward?

Notice the Deliverance of God

They made the right decision. They took the gamble to go forward. When by faith you and I decide to move forward, God will honor your faith and make a way, when we think there is no way. Look at what God did when they exercised their faith to move forward. 2 Kings 7:5-7 God made the Syrians to hear horses and chariots coming upon them, and they were scared to death, got up and fled. You may have a wagon full of doubts,but Jesus said if we have the faith of a grain of a mustard seed, we can move mountains . Don't compare yourself to other Christians that you think are more spiritual than you . You don't know where another person is in their walk with God. Trust God and decide that every day you are going forward. Some days it might be an inch or a mile. God is not interested so much in how far forward you go. He just wants to see you by faith, making forward progress. And if God be for us who can be against us? GLORY !

Notice the Delights of the Camp

In 2 Kings 7:8 we get the picture of Innie, Mennie, Miny, and Moe, who by faith moved forward. God had sent the noise of war horses and chariots, and the Syrians had fled. They went into the city and sure enough they had a feast. No doubt they took off the leper rags and put on the clothes that had been left behind. God honored the lepers' faith and met their needs. Dear reader, O how God wants us to never go back and to never sit still. Take a hold of his mighty hand and though the enemy may try to cut off your food, get on a good spiritual diet. Innie, Minnie, Miny and Moe got every need met. And all because they decided forward was the best gamble. And as my friend years ago at Liberty University, Dr. Sumner Wemp would say "Well Glory!"

14

THE DAY LEFTY
HIT FATTY

JUDGES 3: 15-30

This to me, is a chapter that I wish everyone in the world would read. Not because of my eloquent way of writing. Not because of my way of writing. Not because of the funny title. I am just an old southern boy, with absolutely no experience in writing a book. But read it for the content of the book and what I want to accomplish in writing. The book of Judges is a very unique book. Joshua was dead and the nation asked who is going up against the Canaanites? God chose Judah to go up and there was a great victory that day. Judges could be the book of sevens. There were seven times Israel went into apostasies. Seven times they were tied up in bondage. There were seven men who rose up and delivered Israel. Now then after the great Joshua dies, the next 300 plus years they were led by judges. One of them was Samson, and what a great story is told there. Right after the death of Joshua, was a godly man named Othniel, who was the first of the judges. And Othniel walked and led the children of Israel with the anointing of the Holy Spirit upon him. It just amazes me why Israel would not have a consistent walk with God. Beloved to have fellowship one day and stop the cycle of fellowship with God the next day, would **be** no way to treat the only hope we have in this life.

The second judge was a man named Ehud, he delivered Israel by killing off old fat Eglon. I just want to bring out four things about this story that I hope will find its way into your heart and soul.

The Dedicated

As I said after the death of Joshua came the time period for over 300 years of being led by judges. Ehud saw what had happened as result of old fat Eglon taking over Israel. We now have a leader sent from the Lord to reestablish the worship of the Lord. Let me say that no nation, no workplace, no state, no home and no church can prosper without Godly men, whose God is the Lord. This United States of America cannot make it without returning back to the Lord. The scriptures say, *"Blessed is the nation whose God is the Lord."* Our nation was rooted and grounded on the Judeo-Christian ethic and the Holy Bible. This fact absolutely runs the liberal and socialist of our country crazy. Again, the Bible says the wicked shall be turned into hell and all nations that forget God. Many of the people that founded this country were not Christians however they respected Christianity and still based their decisions on the Word of God. If we had a map of events that led our country, you would find things slowly over a long period of time, pull us away from the Bible as a solid base to govern on. The reason this nation was born in the first place, was to keep us free to worship when, where and how we want to. I am appalled over the fact that Muslims are in our country and many serve in our government. But if you stuff a rag down their erroneous beliefs, it may not be long before that same rag would choke out Christianity also. When one evil wicked woman removed prayer out of school, the saved should have marched by the droves on Washington. But we swept it under the rug and did absolutely nothing but pass the buck down to the government. Then the sin to end all sins was enacted when this supposedly, Christian nation, said it was O.K. to murder the life of a child. Our nation just opened itself up for free-love homosexuality, lesbians, transgender operations, and they even want it all to be legal. We became materialistic in the late fifties and early sixties. We needed two cars, then three cars, out doing the Joneses which has an effect in our homes, moms now have to work too. I am not saying it is a sin for women to have a career, if that is what they want. I am saying that children received negative results because the baby-sitter was TV and video games. Slowly like eyes getting used to the dark, and anything people wanted to do, was all right as long as it did not hurt anyone or anything. Then there were some Godly men who stood up to say that these things were wrong and sin. But by that time, we were playing catch up with sin and the devil. And rather than Christianity being respected, we were laughed at and even accused as being the cause of the world's ills. Men like Jerry Falwell, Charles Stanley, Adrian Rogers, along with Franklin and Billy Graham, began a movement of getting us back to a righteous nation. That sparked a nation of Godly men in local pulpits, that began to change things. They knew the truth in God's word *"blessed is the nation whose God is their Lord."* But when it seemed as though we might be making some head way, we had the Jim Baker and Jimmy Swaggart scandal. These two scandals hurt the cause of Christ so much. It seemed like everyone turned against what they called organized religion. Our nation has been too long getting fat on sin. One sin back forty years ago, was for two people to live together without the benefit of marriage. Living together was adultery. If it was a sin forty years ago it is still sin today. God's standards have not changed. But living together without marriage, as it seems been an accepted lifestyle. Just like Ehud, we need a man of God who will stand up and not be fearful from the blight of sin. Give us more Moody's, raise up more Spurgeon's and just a multitude of men who do not care about being popular to people. Give us some with iron throats and leather lungs that will call sin just what it is, sin. Your name is not the name that ought to be applauded, but it is the name of Jesus.

The Dagger

We as believers have at our disposal the single most powerful weapon against sin. That is the word of God. John *1:1 (KJV) "In the beginning was the word, and the word was with God and the word was God."* Before the beginning of the universe there was God and the word of God. Look at Hebrews 4:12 (KJV) *"For the word of God is quick and powerful and sharper than any two edged sword piercing eve n to the dividing asunder of soul and spirit, and of the joints and marrow, and is a discerner of the thoughts and intents of the heart."* Judges 3 :16 (KJV) says *"But Ehud made him a dagger which had two edges..."* God's eternal word knew everything about you and will convict the very inside of you and me. But it has two edges, and the word of God can also give us victory in the midst of this evil and wicked world. I would like to show you just how important the word of God is. Paul wrote Philippians 2 :9-11 that everyone should bow at the name of Jesus. In order to be saved you should bow at the name of Jesus. However, on this side of eternity the name should be bowed unto. Isaiah 45:23 (KJV) tells us that one day says one day "every knee SHALL bow" to his name. On this side of eternity, we should bow down to his name. If you do not bow to that name now, one day at the Great White Throne Judgment you SHALL bow to his name. So, we can deduct from the word, that the name of Jesus is the supreme name of all names. But look at what David said in Psalms 138: 2 (KJV)*"I will worship toward thy holy temple and praise thy name. For thy loving kindness and for thy truth for thou hast magnified thy word above all they name."* Can you imagine that the name of Jesus is so powerful that all people will bow down to his name? Yet here David says thy word is to be magnified above his name! What a revelation. That yes there is something sweet, calming, secure, and gentle about the name of Jesus. But David says that above that precious name of Jesus is his word. Ehud went into the party to give old fat Eglon a present. Eglon went to his summer parlor. Ehud had his sharp two-edged sword at his right thigh. And with his left hand, because he was a Benjamite, he took the sword, drew it from his right side. Eglon stood up and Ehud thrust his dagger into the belly of old fatty Eglon. He was so fat that Ehud could not even pull the dagger out. Eventually Eglon died and Ehud escaped through a series of doors and roads. And the land had rest for the next forty years.

The Dirt

The Bible records that dirt started to come out of Eglon's belly after being stabbed by Ehud. Literally his bowels were cut by the two-edged sword and dirt came running out. And for sure septicemia would set up a deadly infection in his blood. This dirt is a type of sin in our lives and the dagger a type of the word of God. Anytime we look into the scriptures in a personal way, it will shine a light on any dirt or sin in your life. Notice what God says in Proverbs 1: 24-28 . A simple way to say this is go ahead and keep your sin going in your life, then when you need me, I will laugh at your calamity. Sin is the only thing that keeps us from sweet fellowship with our Lord. All sin was dealt with at the cross. Sin divides us from our daily walk and time with the Lord. James 4:17 (ESV) *"Therefore to him that knows to do good and does it not, to him it is sin."* James 1;14 *"But every man is tempted when he is drawn away of his own lust and enticed."* That is what happened when Adam and Eve fell in the garden of Eden. God said to them, I believe on one of his walks, you have this garden to eat and to do whatever you want. But don't eat of the tree of knowledge of Good and Evil. And you know the rest of the story. Man has had to deal with the dirt of sin ever since. And yes, God hates sin, but his beloved son, Jesus Christ, defeated sin on the cross. Out of dirt grows the weeds of sinfulness.

The Deliverer

God once again sends someone to deliver his people. Ladies and gentlemen, we have a great deliverer in Jesus Christ. If God would be willing to save a man like Adolf Hitler and Eglon, then God would deliver his children when we stray from the fold. We must get back to where we hate sin and know personally, that man Jesus, who had to be beaten, whipped with cat of nine tails, smote, spit upon, crowned with thorns, scorned and ridiculed, and slapped in his face. Then came the crucifixion between two common criminals. Spiritually this story says to me, that the dirt of sin will make the flesh fat. And we need to kill the old man. Look careful y at Galatians 2:20 (KJV) "I am crucified with Christ; nevertheless I live, yet not I, but Christ liveth in me and the life I now live in the flesh, I live by the faith of the son of God, who loved me and gave himself for me." Rather than allowing dirt to build up in us, let us allow the person of the living Christ, in the person of the Holy Spirit live in us. And each day allow the dagger to find those places of sin in us. But remember that our deliverer is Jesus Christ, plus nothing and minus nothing.

15

I'VE LEFT MY PEA PATCH FOR THE LAST TIME

2 SAMUEL :8-12

When I was in the sixth grade at good old Riverside, Virginia, every day at recess there was this boy, I will call Fuzzy. Fuzzy would sneak up behind me and hit me in the head with his fist. No matter what it happened in the morning recess or afternoon recess, Fuzzy would do his dirty deed. I was a nervous wreck every day I went to school. Because I knew that I was going to get beat up again and again. And to top it off, he said if I told on him, he would do even worse to me. This went on for one month. I was ashamed to tell my dad and mom. I was also the new boy from Pennsylvania at the school. I had no friends to ask for help. Finally, another boy, who became a lifelong friend, said you have to deal with Fuzzy or else he will not stop picking on you. My new friend said, I will keep my eye on this guy Fuzzy. When he tries to sneak up, you turn around and hit him in the nose, the blood will scare him, and problem solved. I did more than that, I picked up a piece of a branch off the ground, got behind a tree, and tried to hide it. I had had it for the last time. I was sick up to my eyeballs of getting beat up every single day I went to school. The plan worked. Just before Fuzzy came toward me, my buddy gave the signal. As he was about to hit me again, I turned around and that piece of wood landed right square on his nose. I mean I clocked him good. Blood was everywhere. Then I told him if you tell on me, I will do this every time we come out for recess. Me and Fuzzy later became friends in high school and all was well. Now dear reader please remember this story because it comes back in play, in the book, a little later.

Most everyone has heard of sumo wrestlers. Two big fat gargantuan Japanese men get in the middle of a ring and the one who gets pushed out is the loser. Picture yourself in the middle of the ring of being a Christian. With you, you have Jesus Christ, the Holy Spirit, and God the Father. Because I have been born-again, he has given us his Holy Word the Bible, guardian angels, our family, church, fruits of the Spirit, friends, maybe children, and parents. We can go on and on with our support systems. However, you and I also have enemies that want to push us out of the blessings that comes from God Almighty. The world, the flesh and the devil, all three have their hearts bent on pushing hard to run you out of what God has blessed you with. We also have the lust of the flesh, lust of the eyes and the pride of life. It's no wonder preachers are quitting and people who at one time served the Lord are dropping like flies. The Christians of today want to be entertained. They want their emotions stirred up and get that fuzzy-wuzzy feeling. Then they walk out and never pick up their Bibles to study, quit praying, stop witnessing and then wonder why God does not bless them more. Be very careful of a church that all they do is tickle your ears and they major on an emotional high. Then you have churches where they are so stiff and formal, if you say amen out loud you must be charismatic. And then you have the churches that are so legalistic, they have more rules than God gave Moses. Would it interest you to know that the great C.H. Spurgeon loved to smoke a cigar? D.L. Moody chewed tobacco every day. Then the legalist will preach how great they were and confine someone to hell if someone in their church if they did those things. That my dear reader is the height of hypocrisy. When we moved to Statesville, North Carolina, we visited many churches and settled in one that was Southern Baptist. I had preachers stop fellowship with me because of that very thing. I believe today what I believed forty-five years ago, and I will support a church that has a ministry for all ages and preaches the word of God. Dear reader anything your enemies can do to push you outside of your circle of blessings, they will do it. Come to Jesus and all your troubles will be over says the TV evangelist. Dear reader come to Jesus and be ready to fight. But the good news is, that God will be with you when the bad times come.

Isaiah 43:2 and 3 (ESV) *says "When you pass through the waters I will be with you and through the rivers they shall not overwhelm you when you walk through fire you shall not be burned and the flame shall not consume you. For I am the Lord your God the holy one of Israel your savior.* "God is saying you may get wet, but you will not drown, and when you go through the fire, you may get hot, but you will not burn. Notice the word "WHEN" he is not saying if, he is saying when. One of the greatest positions a man could have was to be in king David's army. He was George Patton of the old testament. He loved and honored his soldiers and they loved and honored king David. In our text we see three men in the army of King David. David is about to die in the middle of a war. These three men are Adino, Eleazer, and Shammah. And we are not talking about the three stooges. These men were strong, vibrant, well trained men. In verse 8 we have a man named Adino. And God's word says he slew eight thousand men with a spear. You say Doug, come on, do you really believe this story? If the Bible said Jonah had swallowed the whale, I would believe it. Either it's all true, or none of it is true. The Bible says, *"Heaven and earth shall pass away, but my words shall not pass away."* Matthew 24:35 (KJV). God's word is the final and only authority for the person who has been washed in the blood of the lamb of God. Next, we have a man named Eleazer who fought so hard his hand clave to the very sword he was using, to fight off the Philistines who were their natural enemy. Imagine for a second how hard you would have to fight for this to happen. Now I want you to look at the third man closer than the other two men. Shammah was in the middle of a garden of lentils that King David had given to him. As much as they fought the Philistines, I would imagine that there were times he got booted out of this pea patch. And that's what all lentils are. They used the lentils in soups and as vegetables. The Bible says he defended it and the Lord gave a great victory that day. I tell you what I think happened. I believe that Shammah had been run out maybe several times by the Philistines. But on that day, with his King dying, he said come on big boys, you have run me out of this pea patch the last time.

CONCLUSION

I hope this book has been a blessing and some help to you . We have a great, big, wonderful God who has saved us eternally. And he loves us the same whether we are walking with him or are in a state of rebellion. When Jesus died, he died for all of us, with all the love he could possibly love with. The cross is our answer to any question we might have. To fathom that the God who with just a word from his mouth, spoke this universe into existence, wants a personal relationship with me, just a dot among all those who have lived, are living and will yet live, is so remarkable and worthy of complete worship, obedience and praise. If I could sum things up, I would simply say what one of the old hymns said "More, more about Jesus." If we walk with him, he promised to never leave us or forsake us. Leave your pea patch for the last time.